Maytag
Handbook
of Good Cooking

Maytag Handbook

An authoritative guide to the kitchen—
from selecting appliances and planning the layout
to the latest approach to efficient food preparation.

Text by *Ann Arnott*

Cover photo and recipes courtesy of the National
Live Stock and Meat Board:
a. Apple-Walnut Cake with Browned Butter Frosting
b. Pork Loin Roast with Spiced Crab Apple Sauce
c. Bacon-Cornbread Dressing
d. Heat circulation in a convection oven

BRIARCLIFF PRESS

Recipe Acknowledgments
Alaska Seafood Marketing Institute: Halibut Division;
American Dairy Association; American Egg Board; American
Sheep Producers Council; American Spice Trade Association;
Hershey Food Corporation; Idaho-Oregon Onion Promotion
Committee; Maryland Office of Seafood Marketing; National
Broiler Council; National Live Stock and Meat Board; National
Pork Producers Council; Oregon-Washington-California Pear
Bureau; Rice Council; United Fresh Fruit and Vegetable
Association.

Library of Congress Catalog
Card Number: 84-72914

ISBN 0-932-52300-5

Published by
BRIARCLIFF PRESS
11 Wimbledon Ct.
Jericho, New York 11753

Printed in the United States of America

Table of Contents

Color Photo Index

Here's where to find the recipes for the dishes shown in the color photographs in the center insert:

Recipe and photo source

Introduction

No cook steps into a kitchen and says "I will now take out my cookbook, which will supply the recipe I will cook from. Next, I will find the foods called for in the recipe, and determine which utensils and equipment I need to prepare the recipe. I will then step to my appliances to cook the food."

Yet cookbooks are written, kitchens are planned, appliance use-and-care manuals are produced, often without taking into account the whole cooking process.

That's why we at The Good Housekeeping Institute were excited to learn of the "Maytag Handbook of Good Cooking." It incorporates the major trends affecting what's happening in the kitchen in a complete, logical and interrelated form.

Best of all, the information is presented in such a way that any cook—or any student of cooking—in any kitchen can enjoy and learn from it. This book should have appeal and be useful to a wide variety of audiences: students, educators, journalists, professional food specialists and—of course—those of us who simply enjoy kitchens and cooking. Both a general index and a recipe index help you quickly find the information you're interested in and then delve as deeply into it as you wish. The content maintains a fine balance of the practical, the technical and simple enjoyment.

A. ELIZABETH SLOAN, PH.D
Director, The Good Housekeeping Institute

How to Use This Book

This book is divided into four sections: Section I, The History of Cooking, is a synopsis of the history, both of cooking and the development of appliances from, literally, the Stone Age to the present time. Few references exist on this subject, particularly in bringing together, in one concise source, the development of appliances in the past 150 years and in how their development affected the preparation of food—and the daily lives of the people preparing it. It is designed to be interesting and enjoyable to the casual reader, and a useful reference for those more interested in this subject.

Section II, Cooking Today, gives detailed information on current cooking appliances and introduces the concept of "Complementary Cooking" to use all of these appliances to full advantage.

This section contains numerous recipes, some of them using only one appliance, others combining the use of several appliances for the best results in preparing a dish (complementary cooking) and several using various appliances to prepare an entire menu (whole meal complementary cooking). The recipes were developed in some of America's most respected test kitchens.

Section III, Kitchen Planning, encompasses the basic tenets of kitchen planning, updated to reflect new lifestyles, appliances and methods of cooking.

Section IV, Appliance Use and Maintenance, pulls together information on what to do about common cooking problems and what to do if an appliance breaks down.

The Table of Contents in the front of the book makes it easy to locate broad coverage of the various topics. The Indices in the back make it easy to locate all detailed coverage (which may be in more than one chapter) of specific items of interest, including recipes.

[1]

The History of Cooking

No one knows for sure when the history of cooking really started, because experts disagree about when fire was "discovered." Generally, it is ascribed to Paleolithic times, or some 750,000 years ago.

Interestingly, the first use of fire was probably for protection, as defense against animals. Cooking itself probably started when one of our forefathers (or mothers, perhaps) discovered that roasting hunks of meat made them taste better than gnawing at them raw. Root vegetables also were made more palatable by cooking.

But cooking food in an open fire often produced mostly charred remains. The next step was to find ways of suspending food above or near the fire to control the rate of cooking—the first "controlled heat." This occurred at least 30,000 years ago. Meat could be suspended above a fire by use of a spit. But remains of cooking vessels dating from at least 25,000 B.C. show that the means had been discovered to cook other types of foods, too.

In Roman times, some 2,000 years ago, there were vast kitchens. Slaves would be going in every

Early cooking innovation

direction from kitchen to dining salon with meat, game, sea-fish, vegetables, fruit and dessert delicacies.

But the equipment was amazingly like what we use today. There were colanders, gridirons, dripping pans and tart dishes.

In Europe in the 14th century—a mere 600 years ago—there were nearly as many gadgets and probably more pots and pans than in a kitchen of today. A "kitchen inventory" at that time included pots, pans, caldrons, pot-hangers, saucepans, wood and metal skewers, spits, meat hooks, larding-needles, mortars, pestles, sieves, strainers, colanders, large and small spoons, cheese graters—and on and on.

Cooking, of course, was still by wood fire, in a fireplace so enormous that an adult could walk in without stooping. Hanging from a hook at the back was a caldron big enough to hold two buckets of water. On hooks and on trivets were pots of different sizes and shapes.

At the front were two great andirons. The uprights of each ended in baskets that could hold pots or jugs to keep the contents warm or to cook. On the front of each upright was a line of hooks to hold scoops, tongs, pokers, forks, skimming ladles and other tools. All had long handles—the heat of the fire necessitated this. Perhaps most important, the hooks supported the roasting spits. The spits were turned by boys, dogs in treadmills or other ingenious devices of the times.

All the kitchen activities were supervised by the cook, who sat nearby in a large chair. Also near the fireplace were such tools and equipment as a bellows to fan the fire, frying pans and—waffle irons!

Turnspit dog

18th century kitchen

Cooking methods didn't really change much from medieval centuries until about the end of the 18th century. A "cooking range" was registered in England in 1780, using coal as the heat source. It required enormous amounts of fuel, however, and created a lot of smoke. Then, Sir Benjamin Thompson, better known as Count Rumford, developed a closed-top range.

It was much more economical in use of fuel—using almost all the heat that a small fire could produce. This brought with it three cooking principles that are still "buzz words" today: Adjustable heat, though of a primitive nature. Energy conservation. And "slow cooking." In the roaster Rumford developed, a tray of water prevented temperatures inside from rising above 212° F. Meat roasted in this, he claimed—and many eminent persons who tried it agreed with him—tasted better, was more highly flavored and much more juicy and delicate than meat roasted before an open fire.

Controlled by flues, dampers and metal plates the new ranges with adjustable heat made preparation of souffles, sauces and sauteed dishes within the scope of any household. As prices of this type of new stove began to drop, more and more cooks acquired them.

This type of iron range probably came into general use in middle-class homes here and abroad in the 1860s. About 20 years later, coal gas became available and the gas-fueled stove started to replace the solid-fuel type.

Range with adjustable heat

ENTERING THE 20TH CENTURY

So, as the 20th century neared, more major changes took place in how cooks could cook and how easily they could do it. The gas-fired stove made possible much more precise heat control—though still primitive by today's standards.

The development of these new-fangled stoves initiated many other changes in kitchen equipment. Frying pans and utensils no longer needed the extra-long handles; cooking vessels didn't need feet to keep them out of the ashes. And the kitchen moved to the house proper—before, it had often been banished to the basement (if there was one) or tacked onto the back of the house.

The fact that oven temperatures could be regulated (and oven thermometers were available) led to changes in the way recipes could be written. Fannie Farmer's *The Boston Cooking-School Cook Book*, originally published in 1896, was one of the first to give precise times and temperatures, rather than saying something like "cook in moderate oven until done."

ENTER GAS STOVES AND ELECTRIC RANGES

Gas stoves caught on slowly at first. In 1859, there were fewer than 100 gas stove users. Even in 1876 at the Centennial Exposition in Philadelphia, pies baked in a gas-fueled oven were considered an oddity. But progress came quickly after that and, by the turn of the century, gas stoves were in common use even in middle-class households.

The first electric kitchen was displayed at the World's Fair (The Columbia Exposition) of 1893 in

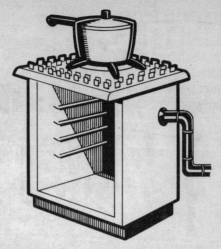

Primitive gas stove

Chicago. But it was nearly 20 years before a reliable electric range was developed.

In 1910, at the National Electric Light Association Convention in St. Louis, the world took notice of an invention by George A. Hughes, a North Dakota newspaperman who had started his own electric company. The invention was an electric cooking device that consisted of heating wires placed in porcelain blocks.

Curiously enough, the unit was called an "electrified gas stove." The name didn't take, but the stove did. Only two years later, 1,000 electric ranges were in use in Billings, Mont. There, the users received a special rate of three cents per kilowatt hour, compared to the regular rate for lights of 30 cents.

Electric range—1900

The earliest gas and electric ranges were adapted from wood-burning or coal-burning stoves. Insulation often consisted simply of a thin piece of asbestos on the oven walls.

Temperature control was introduced in 1915 when a thermostat for a gas water heater was adapted to a gas range. Pilot lights, for automatic lighting of gas stoves, began to appear in the early 1900s. (Pilot lights, now, of course, are being replaced by fuel-saving electric ignition devices.)

The location of the oven kept shifting—then, as now, there was no consensus on which was the best spot. At first it usually was below the cooking surface. Later, legs were added to the stoves and the oven was placed alongside the surface cooking area.

Then it was moved below again and a second unit was added at eye level—one of the first of these was introduced in 1908. It also had a storage compartment from which hot water could be drawn at the turn of a faucet.

The early stoves, like Henry Ford's cars, were first available in a choice of colors—so long as it was black. Eventually, techniques were developed for fusing porcelain enamel to steel, and by 1925 stoves with white exteriors had become quite popular.

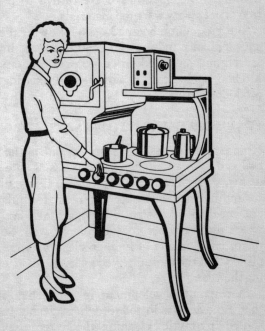

1930s range

THE 1920S TO 1940S

Through the 1920s and 1930s, improvements continued gradually. Double ovens, choices of colors and styles, improvements in insulation, smaller models (30-inch, 24-inch and even 20-inch models) and more precise timers and controls were among important refinements that helped push sales of gas ranges to 11 million and electric types to two million during the depression of the 1930s.

Almost no appliances were produced during World War II. Appliance factories, like most other manufacturing facilities, were turned to production of necessary wartime materials.

But production boomed again following the war. The appliance industry poured huge sums into research and produced an entire new generation of kitchen appliances, in addition to exciting new product features.

POST WORLD WAR II TO PRESENT

From earliest times, clean-up was one of the most disliked parts of kitchen work. Sales of automatic dishwashers began to take off in the 1950s, thanks to improvements in both detergent formulations and mechanical design of the machines, and food waste disposers became popular as well. So two major components of kitchen clean-up were simplified. But the most disliked task remained, cleaning the oven.

A startling development in 1963 changed all that. An oven was introduced that "cleaned itself." Called "pyrolytic" cleaning, the system uses very high temperatures (approximately 900°F) during a special separate cycle to reduce the soil in the oven to a small amount of ash that can be easily wiped away. The extra insulation required because of the high temperatures during cleaning also made these electric ovens more efficient when used at normal cooking temperatures.

Then the "catalytic" or continuous cleaning oven was introduced just a few years later. With this system, used on both gas and electric ranges, soil is reduced through catalytic action to a presentably clean condition during normal baking or broiling. (See Chapter 2 for more detailed information on how the systems operate.)

Other features for easier range cleaning included tops designed to contain spills, pull-off control knobs, removable reflector pans and plug-in elements. Manual oven cleaning is made easier by bake elements that tilt up and out of the way, and lift-off oven doors.

Plug-in elements

Through all this, the kitchen was changing its looks too. The kitchen of the 1950s has been described as "cheerfully antiseptic." Appliances, if not white, were one of the pastel colors popular in kitchen decor then—pink, yellow or aqua. The renewed interest in food and cooking hadn't yet begun. The fascination, in fact, was with the new food technology of frozen foods and dinners, and the kitchen was a sort of laboratory. Time and motion studies were being done—resulting in some of the precepts of kitchen planning that remain valid today.

In the 1960s, appliances and cabinets shifted in design from soft, rounded lines to more squared-off, angular ones. Wood tones became important, and appliance colors such as coppertone and avocado were introduced. In the late 1970s, tastes shifted again, this time to warmer colors including almond.

But much more dramatic changes were taking place in cooking appliances. In the 1960s and 1970s, entirely new types of cooking products were introduced—or becoming popular.

Perhaps no other cooking appliance opened up as many new cooking options for the consumer as the microwave oven.

The discovery of the cooking principle used in the microwave oven is an interesting tale in itself:

A chocolate bar melted in Dr. Percy Spencer's pocket for no apparent reason. The year was 1946 and Dr. Spencer was working with high-frequency radio waves generated by a vacuum tube—called a magnetron, and an essential component of radar and other microwave devices.

Dr. Spencer wondered if there was a relationship

between radar waves and the melted chocolate. Soon, his work and others proved that there was— his experimenting led to the discovery that these waves can, indeed, penetrate food and create cooking action. (For details on how this cooking principle works, see Chapters 2 and 5.)

The first microwave ovens were used in commercial and institutional applications. Prices were $500 to $1,000 or more. The first microwave unit designed for the residential market (designed to fit into a 24-inch oven cabinet) was introduced in 1955. However, these weighed 1,000 lbs. and required a 220-volt outlet, so they weren't practical.

In the early 1960s, a double-oven range was introduced, with one of the ovens modified for microwave cooking as well as conventional baking and broiling. In 1967, the first "portable" microwave oven was introduced. While not easily portable because of size and weight, it did not require permanent installation or special wiring.

Microwave oven technology, features and competition, began to move rapidly after that. The first countertop models had only one power level and did not offer such options as automatic defrost, temperature probes or programmed cooking. (For a review of features and types of microwave ovens available today, see Chapter 2.)

In 1961, the first down-draft range was introduced. It incorporated a surface ventilation system that eliminated the need for an overhead exhaust hood, and also provided improved ventilation capability. Smoke and cooking odors are captured at the cooking surface and pulled down through the vent and then through ductwork to the outdoors.

The indoor grilling feature of the electric range was introduced in 1967.

In 1963, the glass-ceramic cooking surface (commonly called a "smooth-top") was introduced.

And, in 1972, the first "convertible cooktop" utilizing the down-draft principle was introduced. These have modules that are easily interchangeable, including standard elements, glass-ceramic smooth-tops and the grill module. Accessories include a griddle, rotisserie, wok and slow cooker. A more recent addition is an induction cooking module—more on that in Chapter 2.

Convection (forced-air circulation ovens) have been used in commercial bakeries and restaurants for many years. But it wasn't until 1973 that the first model designed for residential use—a countertop model—was introduced in the United States. Countertop models are still available, sometimes in conjunction with a microwave oven. Since 1976, they have been available as part of a gas or electric oven, offering the option of convection or conventional (radiant heat) cooking.

[2]

Cooking Appliances: Current Options and Technology

Improvements in cooking appliances are being made continuously. Some are almost invisible—a better gasket or door seal for greater energy efficiency; a new material that makes a part last longer. Others are more dramatic —microwave cooking or induction cooking. Since purchasing a major cooking appliance is not an everyday event, it's hard to stay current on what's available. This chapter is an up-to-date look at the cooking appliance market. Some general trends that apply across the board are followed by detailed information on individual products.

GENERAL APPLIANCE TRENDS

Certain trends apply to cooking appliances in general. Here are the most important ones:

Solid-state Electronics The most obvious application of this technology is in controls on microwave ovens and other appliances. The touch-control pads are sleek and modern; easy to set and easy to clean. And they're highly accurate in controlling time and temperature.

But, with solid state, beauty is much more than skin deep—the major benefits lie beneath the surface. Solid state, microprocessor chips eliminate the need for many behind-the-scene parts (wheels, gears and electrical contacts) making controls much more compact.

Self-diagnostic servicing is an increasingly important function of solid-state applications. When something goes awry, the chip will indicate what is wrong so that a service technician—or the owner, in some cases—will quickly know which repairs to make.

Expect to see more solid-state technology in cooking appliances. In fact, because there is so much the microchip control can do, the appliance designer is challenged with the opportunity to provide the consumer with still more benefits.

Energy Usage   Modern cooking appliances are energy-efficient. However, the amount of energy used depends on the user's habits. Energy usage also can be substantially affected by the type of cooking appliance. Microwave ovens, convection ovens and induction cooktops all offer energy savings over conventional methods of cooking the same foods.

Quality   Modern consumers demand quality when they shop for major appliances. That's partially due to the consumer movement that raised people's awareness of the value of product quality. Busy lifestyles, too, have taught consumers that appliances that last longer and need fewer repairs make life easier.

CONVENTIONAL RANGES—
GAS AND ELECTRIC

Conventional gas and electric ranges have served cooks' needs well for many years, and will continue to do so. The term "range" is used here to include the many different configurations of conventional gas and electric cooking appliances. The most popular type (of all cooking appliances) remains the 30-inch range, incorporating oven, broiler and cooktop in a single appliance. It may either be "free-standing," or designed as a "drop-in" or "slide-in," for a built-in look. Although 30-inch is the standard width, other sizes are available. Conventional ranges also are available with a second oven at eye level; or as separate units—a built-in cooktop and a single or double wall oven.

All-in-one ranges take up the least space—good for a compact kitchen. But separate cooktop and oven can offer more flexibility in kitchen design. Since foods in a conventional oven typically take far less "tending" than those on the cooktop, being able to separate the two functions usually leads to a kitchen that is easier to work in.

Conventional ranges also can incorporate a microwave or convection oven, a grill or a smooth-top cooking surface. See other sections in this chapter for details.

Here are some convenience and construction features to look for in conventional gas and electric ranges, cooktops and wall ovens:

Controls
These may be rotary dials, pushbuttons or elec-

tronic touch pads. Look for easy-clean design—
control dials should be removable. Depending on
design, controls may be at the front of the range, on
a back panel or in some double-oven ranges, in a
single control panel at one side of the upper oven.

Programmable controls make it possible to set
the oven to cook at a later time, to operate a self-
cleaning cycle during off-peak energy-use hours or
to automatically switch to "holding" temperature
at the end of a preset cooking time. Electronic
digital clocks and oven timers offer cooking convenience.

Surface Units

For easy cleaning, look for: electric elements that
lift up or unplug, with removable drip bowls beneath; removable gas burners and burner grates;
one-piece cooktop construction, with raised rim to
contain spills; lift-up tops for easy cleaning of the
area under the cooktop.

Electric Cooktops normally have both six-inch
and eight-inch elements; either two of each or three
six-inch and one eight-inch for bigger cooking jobs.
Usually the eight-inch element has a higher wattage rating for fast heating of larger pans or quantities of food.

Gas Cooktops have burners with infinite flame
adjustment. Some have "click-stop" positions at
high, medium and low for easier setting. Cooktops
with automatic, electric or electronic ignition eliminate constantly burning pilot lights and not only
save energy but keep the kitchen cooler.

Lift-up gas cooktop

Ovens

Probably the most important point to consider is the type of oven cleaning system. Here are the three types and how they work:

Self-cleaning (pyrolytic) Ovens use temperatures above normal baking temperatures (approximately 900°F) to automatically clean the entire oven. The cycle, which lasts from two to three hours, eliminates soil completely or reduces it to a gray, powdery ash that is easily wiped off with a damp cloth. These ovens use a special porcelain enamel and a special door seal, and generally have heavier insulation around the top and sides and in the door for more efficient operation during the clean cycle as well as during regular use.

Broiler pans should be cleaned by hand; oven racks can be cleaned automatically in most ovens, but they will become discolored and can be difficult to slide in and out of the oven. Heavy spill-overs and grease deposits will be removed during the self-clean cycle. In most cases the area outside the door gasket must be cleaned manually.

A self-cleaning oven is more economical to use than other types of ovens for two reasons: The extra insulation makes the oven more efficient in energy use during normal operation; and the modest cost to operate the self-cleaning cycle during the course of a year probably is less than what would be spent on a commercial oven cleaner.

Continuous Cleaning (catalytic) Ovens are designed to always keep the oven presentably clean. This type of oven has a rough porous texture. When grease spatters on these specially treated walls, it spreads out and is partially absorbed. Then, heat and natural air currents through the oven, combined with the catalytic surface, help the spatter burn off during normal oven use.

The higher the oven temperature, the faster the cleaning action. The time involved will vary from a few minutes to several hours, depending on the type of soil, the amount or size of soil, the oven temperature and the length of time the oven is in use.

In some ovens, the special coating is not applied to the oven bottom or door, so these areas must be cleaned by hand. In other ovens, all interior surfaces are coated.

Manual Cleaning Ovens have a porcelain enamel finish that is smooth and durable. While the surfaces do require manual cleaning, there are a number of oven features that can make cleaning

Lift-up baking element

easier. These include rounded corners, so that there are no crevices where soil can collect; a baking element that tilts up and out of the way to make it easier to clean the oven bottom; a removable broiler reflector plate that not only improves broiling efficiency, but shields the top of the oven from spatters and can be removed for easy cleaning; a lift-off oven door to make it easier to reach the oven interior, and a removable oven bottom that can be taken right to the sink for cleaning.

Other oven features:

Temperature Probes These monitor internal food temperatures; shut off automatically and signal when the food has reached the selected doneness.

Broiling In an electric range, this is done at the top of the oven under a high-wattage element. In gas ovens, the broiler compartment is most often under the oven burner, but some have a radiant heat broiler at the top of the oven cavity.

Oven Window Makes it possible to check cooking progress without wasting energy by opening the door.

CONVECTION OVENS

In convection cooking, a fan continuously circulates heated air in the oven while foods are cooking. This is not a new cooking principle. In Europe, convection ovens have been standard equipment for commercial as well as residential use for years. Commercial bakeries and restaurants have been using convection ovens in the United States for more than 30 years because more food can be placed in the ovens side-to-side and top-to-bottom, yet still achieve even baking results. Large quantities of frozen food can be rapidly reconstituted and prepared foods reheated quickly. In addition, convection ovens provide high-quality roasting and baking.

Here's how a convection oven differs from a conventional oven: The cooking process in either a convection or conventional (radiant heat) oven depends on gradual conduction of heat from the outside of the food to the center. In a conventional oven the air is almost static. In a convection oven, power driven, heated air strips away the layer of cold air surrounding the food. The heated air continually surrounds the food, thereby increasing the speed at which heat is conducted into the food.

Convection ovens are available in electric ranges and in built-in ovens and offer the option of either convection or conventional cooking. They also are available in gas models. There also are microwave-convection ovens and countertop convection ovens.

Advantages

Faster Cooking   This is particularly true for

Convection oven currents

large foods or large quantities of food. For example, a 12-pound turkey will roast in about three hours in a convection oven, but requires about four hours in a radiant oven.

Larger Quantity Cooking Because better air circulation provides more even heat distribution for even baking results, more food can be placed in the oven—side-to-side or top-to-bottom. Three sheets of cookies can be baked at one time or as many as five loaves of bread on one rack. This is a real advantage for large families, those individuals who like to bake in large quantities and those who entertain frequently.

Convection baking

Energy Savings   When larger quantities of food are cooked at one time, or shorter cooking times are required, the oven obviously isn't on as long, thus saving energy. Also, preheating generally is not necessary, because the hot air begins the heating process almost immediately and heats the oven interior very quickly.

Quality of Certain Foods   Bread products, in particular, are crustier and golden brown.

INDUCTION COOKTOPS

Induction cooking uses electromotive force to heat cookware made of magnetic materials (such as iron, nickel, steel or various alloys). The hot cooking utensil then cooks the food. The cooktop surface itself stays cooler than the cooking utensil.

Experimenting with induction cooking began as early as 1890. However, recent technology (such as solid-state circuitry) is just now making induction cooktops practical for home use.

The induction principle has been used for many years in industry to heat treat or melt metals. Solutions to reducing component size and cost had to be found before it was feasible for home use. It is more expensive than conventional electric coil cooking units.

Several companies now are selling induction cooktops and they also are available as a two-unit, plug-in cartridge for convertible cooktops and grill-ranges.

How Induction Cooking Works   Induction cooktops look much like smooth-top cooktops and may be either light or dark in color, but there the similarity ends. Under the cooktop (normally glass-ceramic) is a coil of wire for each cooking surface area. Each coil has a solid-state power supply. When the controls are turned on, electric current to the coils is converted to high frequency alternating current. This current flows through the coil, creating an alternating magnetic field. When a ferrous metal (such as cast iron or steel) utensil is in place, the current flows through the utensil. (It is an induced current—therefore it is induction cooking.) It is the hot utensil that cooks the food. The intensity of the alternating magnetic field can be varied by the cooktop's control.

The glass-ceramic used for the cooktop's surface is transparent to the current and is unaffected by it since it does not contain ferromagnetic materials. Therefore, it is heated only by transfer of heat from the cooking utensil and remains relatively cool.

Advantages

Fast Response and Control Starts and stops cooking immediately—can quickly stop boil-overs. It has infinite temperature range with instant response in increasing and decreasing cooking temperatures. Precise low-heat control permits cooking delicate foods without burning.

Energy Efficient Uses no more energy than needed to heat the size of utensil being used. It has highest ratio of BTUs produced to energy used of any electric cooktop. Unit shuts off if no utensil is on the cooktop. Less heat escapes into the kitchen (only the cooking utensil and food are heated—not the entire cooking surface).

Easier Clean-up Because of cooler surface, spills do not burn on.

SURFACE VENTILATION RANGES AND COOKTOPS

In 1961, the first range to use built-in ventilation (sometimes called "proximity" ventilation) was introduced. This range diverted smoke, grease and cooking odors from the cooking surface through a vent and then through ductwork to the outdoors.

Surface ventilation offers several advantages over previous choices.

Advantages

More Effective Ventilation The central location draws smoke from all areas of the cooktop—from front to back on either side. This system has many times the "capture velocity" of a hood of similar power located at a typical height above the cooking surface. The drawing compares the effectiveness of the surface ventilation and overhead hood systems.

Because the surface ventilation is closer to the source of steam, smoke, grease and odors they are removed more effectively. Farther away from the surface, less removal takes place. When an overhead hood is used, the maximum ventilation is located near the hood and the exhaust system is less efficient.

Easier Cleaning The permanent filter found in most surface ventilation ranges and cooktops lifts out easily for sink or dishwasher cleaning. The location of an overhead hood and filters makes cleaning an awkward chore—one that many owners seldom attempt.

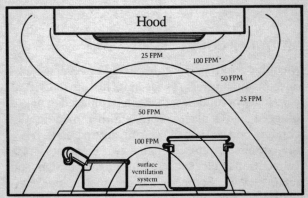

* Feet per minute

Capture velocity comparison

Location Flexibility   The location of the down-draft range or cooktop or the size of the room has little effect on the performance of the ventilation system. This offers greater flexibility in designing kitchens. The range or cooktop can be installed in an island or peninsula, making the kitchen more open—a definite trend in kitchen design.

Indoor Grilling   Of course, a major advantage of surface ventilation is the use of an indoor grill. Indoor grilling would have been impossible without the development of surface ventilation systems.

In the first grill-ranges, the grill was a permanent part of the range. The cooktop consisted of two conventional surface units on one side and the grill on the other. While cooks loved the indoor grilling feature, having only two conventional cooking elements was limiting at times. That led to the introduction of the first "convertible" or "modular" cooktops.

MODULAR COOKTOPS

Modular cooktops now are offered by several appliance manufacturers. These units feature individual cartridges or modules, that can be plugged in or unplugged and replaced with another module, depending on the type of cooking desired. Each module, in effect, replaces half—two elements—of a conventional electric cooktop. Exact design and features vary. Some of the options include conventional, two-unit electric module; grill; griddle; a slow or deep cooker; rotisserie accessory; glass-ceramic module; wok; canner and induction module. (For additional information on these cooktops, see Chapter 3.)

MICROWAVE OVENS

It is difficult to think of a cooking appliance that has opened up new ways of cooking and changed people's cooking habits as much as a microwave oven. Because this cooking concept is still so new to many people, the first part of this discussion contains detailed technical information. The latter part deals with the current state of the art—microwave oven types and features available.

What is Microwave Energy?

Microwaves are a form of energy similar to radio, CB, TV, light and infrared waves. Although they can't be seen, felt or touched, their effects are well known. For example, radio, CB or TV waves are around us all the time, light waves can be seen and the warmth or heat of infrared waves can be felt.

Collectively, these high frequency electromagnetic energy waves are called radiant energy because they travel or radiate outward in a wave-like motion until they lose their energy and dissipate. This movement is similar to the movement of waves on a pond when the surface is disturbed by a pebble.

Radiant energy travels at the speed of light (186,282 miles per second) and in a wave-like motion. The length of the wave can vary from several miles like some radio waves to a billionth of an inch. Radiant energy disappears instantly when its source of production stops. For example, when you turn off the light switch, there are no lingering light waves to help you find your way to bed. And, when the microwave oven turns off, there are no lingering microwaves to continue cooking. When production stops, radiant energy ceases immediately.

Principles of Microwave Energy

When microwaves come in contact with an object, they will react in one of three ways, just like light waves from the sun:

Reflect   When microwaves come in contact with metal, such as the metal oven walls, the metal screen in the window of the door, aluminum foil or metal cooking utensils, the energy will reflect or bounce off the metal just as sunlight reflects off a shiny metal object. This is why metal utensils generally should not be used in a microwave oven— metal will reflect the microwave energy away from the food and no cooking will take place. This also is the reason the oven walls and the screen in the window are made of metal. The metal reflects microwaves and prevents them from escaping the oven.

Pass Through   Microwaves will pass through most glass, paper or plastic materials, just as sunlight passes through a glass windowpane, as if the material wasn't there. Therefore, these materials do not become hot. This is one of the reasons why microwave cooking is called "cool cooking." Although the foods cooked in a microwave oven get hot, in many cases the dish and the oven stay cool. If the dish or oven does become warm, the warmth comes from heat transferred from the food rather than from the microwave energy.

Absorb Food, or to be more exact, sugar/fat/water molecules in the food, absorb microwave energy. As the molecules absorb more and more energy, they quickly begin to move faster and faster until they are moving at the speed of two billion, four hundred fifty million cycles per second (2450 megahertz). As the molecules move, they rub against each other causing friction. This friction produces heat and cooking begins. Rubbing your hands together produces heat by much the same type of friction.

How Microwaves Produce Heat in Food

As the molecules of the food absorb microwaves, they begin to move rapidly, causing friction, and in turn create heat. Absorption is below the surface of the food, not at the surface as in conventional cooking. Therefore, heat quickly builds up in the outer layers and then, like conventional cooking only much faster, begins to conduct to the center of the food. The depth of the energy absorption depends on the density and composition of the food. The fast penetration and absorption of microwaves gives microwave cooking its primary benefit—speed.

Conventional cooking is an indirect way of cooking because heat is transferred from one medium to another. When cooking in a conventional gas or electric oven, the oven air must first be preheated. This can take from five to 20 minutes, depending upon the temperature selected. When food is placed in the oven, the hot oven air slowly begins to penetrate and heat the outer surface of the food. As the outer surface becomes hotter and hotter, the heat slowly begins to conduct or spread to the center of the food.

Microwave cooking is a direct method of cooking because heat is created directly within the food itself. As soon as the microwave oven is turned on, food immediately begins to absorb energy.

How a Microwave Oven Works

An easy way to understand the operation of a microwave oven is to compare it with a radio station. A radio station creates radio waves, then broadcasts or sends the waves through the air to a home, an office or car. When the radio is turned on, the radio receiver converts or changes the radio waves into sound.

The same thing happens in a microwave oven. But, instead of sending waves out over a great distance, it all happens in a small metal box—the oven. The microwave oven is simply a metal box containing a miniature, self-contained radio broadcasting system. When the microwave oven is turned on the magnetron tube sends or broadcasts microwaves through the wave guide into the oven. The receiver in this case is the food. When the food "receives the microwave energy," it converts the energy into heat and cooking begins.

While microwave ovens are designed in different ways, the drawing on this page and the accompanying explanation describe basic components.

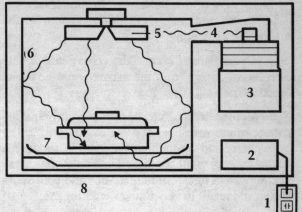

1. 115V outlet   5. Metal Stirrer
2. Transformer   6. Metal Cavity
3. Magnetron Tube   7. Glass Tray
4. Metal Wave Guide   8. Oven Bottom

1. 115V Outlet   Unless it is part of a conventional oven or range, a microwave oven operates on standard grounded household current of 115V. However, it is recommended that the microwave oven have its own separate circuit.

2. Transformer   The transformer increases the power of the household current by stepping up the voltage to a level that is acceptable to the magnetron tube.

3. Magnetron Tube   The magnetron tube is the heart of the microwave oven. Its function is to convert household electrical energy with a frequency of 60hz into microwave energy with the frequency of 2450mhz. It is a vacuum tube that produces very short electromagnetic waves.

The magnetron tube directs, or broadcasts, the newly converted energy from the magnetron tube toward the wave guide.

4. Metal Wave Guide   The wave guide directs microwave energy from the magnetron tube to the oven cavity.

5. Metal Stirrer   A stirrer or antenna helps distribute microwave energy more evenly within the oven cavity and throughout the food. Without this device, energy would be directed to only a few areas in the oven. This would create hot and cold spots and would result in very uneven cooking.

6. Metal Cavity   The oven cavity is made of steel (sometimes covered with another material). As microwave energy enters the oven, it reflects off the metal walls and floor and is absorbed by the food. Cooking begins at this point.

7. Glass Tray   A glass tray at the bottom (sometimes built in) is designed to allow microwave energy to pass through the tray to the food. If removable, it must be in place whenever the oven is in use. If food is placed directly on the metal oven floor, microwave energy will not be able to cook the underside of the food. This will result in uneven cooking.

8. Oven Bottom   The true oven bottom or floor is located under the removable glass tray or other base. The purpose of this space is to elevate food off the metal oven floor to allow microwave energy to penetrate the underside of the food for fast, even cooking results.

Advantages

Cooks Faster   With a microwave oven it is possible to cook up to 80 percent of the foods you normally prepare in less than 50 to 75 percent of the time it would take to cook the same foods conventionally.

Here are some examples:

Food	Conventional Cooking	Microwave Cooking
Meatloaf	1¼ to 1½ hours	14 to 17 minutes
Ham & Scalloped Potatoes	1½ to 1¾ hours	38 to 53 minutes
Baked Chicken 2–3½ lbs.	1 to 1¾ hours	12 to 24 minutes
Baked Potatoes (4)	1 hour	12 to 16 minutes
Pineapple Upside-Down Cake	30 to 45 minutes	5 to 7 minutes

Cooks Better   Some foods cooked in a microwave oven retain more color, flavor and nutritional value than conventionally cooked foods because they cook with little or no water and in a short period of time.

Reheating   With a microwave oven leftovers become planned-overs, which can be reheated quickly and easily without a "leftover" taste or appearance.

Defrosting With a microwave oven it is possible to defrost in a matter of minutes automatically. Microwave defrosting is a unique benefit for there is no other appliance that offers this feature.

Shortens Clean-Up Time It is estimated that about 1½ hours per day can be saved in clean-up time alone when using a microwave oven. Here are several reasons why this is true:

• Foods that spatter such as bacon can be covered with paper towels to help keep oven soiling to a minimum. If the oven does become soiled, the soil will not bake on as in conventional cooking, for microwave cooking is cool cooking. A damp cloth or sponge will clean the oven—no messy oven cleaners or steel wool pads to contend with.

• Glass trays in some ovens will catch and hold a boil-over. Just take the glass shelf to the sink for cleaning.

• For many types of cooking the oven and dish will stay cool, thus food will not bake on the dish or oven. Dishes (especially those used for macaroni and cheese, roasts, bacon, oatmeal or milk-based foods such as pudding) will be much easier to clean, either at the sink or in the dishwasher.

• Since no metal pots and pans are used, just glass, plastic or paper, the cooking utensils are either cleaned in the dishwasher or thrown away. No messy scouring to do after cooking.

• Also contributing to easy clean-up is the ability to use one dish for many functions, thus cutting down on the number of dishes to wash. For example, use a glass casserole dish to prepare and cook the food, then either freeze for later use or use the same dish to serve in. If there are any leftovers, just refrigerate them and reheat the next day—all in the same casserole dish.

Cooler   Foods cooked in a microwave oven get hot, yet in most cases the oven and the cooking utensil remain cool. Unlike a conventional oven, you can open the door of a microwave oven to check cooking without having hot air escaping to heat up the kitchen.

Limitations of Microwave Cooking

Microwave ovens are popular because they cook many foods quickly and with excellent results. Fruits and vegetables are especially well prepared in a microwave oven and leftovers come out tasting like the first time around. But some foods are better prepared on the range or in the conventional or convection oven. For example, when browning is desired as with breads, cookies and some meats such as roasts and chops, the conventional or convection oven is a better choice unless the microwave oven has a built-in browning element. Conventional range-top cooking is a better choice for pasta and rice, too, because there's no time advantage to preparing them in the microwave oven. That's also true for large quantities of food. Some dishes, such as fruit-filled pies and frozen meats, can be started in a microwave oven and finished in a conventional or convection oven with excellent results and efficient use of the best qualities of more than one cooking appliance.

MODERN MICROWAVE OVENS

From the original microwave ovens that offered essentially an on/off switch and one power level—full speed ahead—microwave ovens now are available in a variety of types, with features to suit nearly every kitchen and cooking preference.

Types of Microwave Ovens

Countertop Microwave Ovens are popular and offer the widest choice of features. They come in various sizes.

There is no standard for either exterior or interior dimensions, nor is it necessarily true that the larger the interior capacity, the larger the exterior dimensions—it depends on brand or design.

If the microwave oven has to fit into a particular spot in the kitchen, be certain to measure all dimensions. If the oven is to be built into a wall cabinet, or otherwise enclosed for a built-in look, it is important to check the venting requirements—for air circulation needed around the sides and back of most ovens. Specification sheets will give details, and most kitchen designers are knowledgeable about such requirements.

Countertop microwave-convection ovens also are available, that can cook with the speed of microwaves, brown and crisp food with convection heat or cook with both methods at the same time.

Over-the-range Microwave Ovens, incorporating a vent hood (that can be ducted or nonducted) and light, are designed to be installed over a range or cooktop, replacing a standard range hood.

Eye-level range

Under-the-cabinet Models are a space-saving variation of 115-volt units. These compact to mid-size units are designed to be hung under a wall cabinet (they also can sit on the countertop) freeing countertop work space below.

Eye-level Ranges are all-in-one ranges with a microwave oven above the cooktop and a gas, electric or gas-convection full-size lower oven.

Combination Ranges   are full-size electric, gas or gas-convection ranges that can cook with microwaves, conventional or convection heat, or a combination of these. The microwave action speeds up the cooking, while still providing traditional browning and crisping.

Built-in Microwave Ovens   also offer a variety of choices. They include a single microwave-only oven, a microwave-convection combination; or a bank of two wall ovens, with a microwave (or microwave-convection) oven above and an electric (conventional or convection-conventional) or gas oven below.

Microwave Oven Features

The only uniform thing about microwave ovens available and their features is that there's no uniformity! Models and features abound. Here are the most common—or most important—features:

Cooking Power The wattage output determines the amount of microwave power available for cooking. Most full-size countertop ovens have a power output of approximately 600 to 700 watts. Cooking times may vary slightly from oven to oven. Compact ovens usually have an output of 400 to 500 watts; cooking times will be somewhat longer.

Power Levels This is an important feature. Just as not all foods benefit from the highest heat setting on range top or oven, neither do all foods benefit from full power in a microwave oven.

Variable power controls make it possible to

adjust the cooking speed to the food being cooked. A lower power setting is needed, for example, for even defrosting of foods, for gentle simmering or for proper reheating. While names and methods of achieving power settings vary, typically a power setting of "1" would provide 10 percent of available cooking power; "4", 40 percent; "10", 100 percent and so forth. In addition, some models have special defrost cycles that automatically lower power levels or cycle to "hold" periods as food thaws, for faster, more even thawing.

Capacity If looking at (or in) microwave ovens for the first time, don't be put off by the fact that they're much smaller than conventional ovens—the two types of ovens are used in quite different ways.

Ovens with the same or similar cubic capacity rating may have quite different internal dimensions. Keep in mind that width and depth usually are more important than height. Be sure that favorite cookware will fit inside—in both directions since dishes often have to be rotated.

Controls Electro-mechanical controls generally are found on less expensive models. They are easy to understand and to set, but are less accurate and versatile than electronic controls. However, they may provide all the flexibility needed for many users. Electronic controls provide more than sleek, good looks. They are highly accurate and perform many other functions. They often give a digital readout of time of day, cooking time, temperature, power level and so on. They may contain preset programs to provide optimum cooking of various types of foods or make it possible for the user to set up programs.

Some control panels are easier to program or to understand than others. This is a point to check when shopping for a microwave oven.

Energy Distribution Early microwave ovens had uneven patterns of energy distribution within the oven, resulting in "hot" and "cool" spots that caused uneven cooking. Various steps have been taken to eliminate this problem. These include stirrer fans, rotating antennas, turntables on which the food sits and designs in which the microwave energy enters the oven from more than one source. While some designs are better than others, in essence, all microwave ovens cook more evenly now than they did when first introduced.

Temperature Probes Ovens with this feature automatically heat foods to a pre-selected temperature. One end of the skewer-like probe goes into the food (a mug of soup, a roast, a casserole) the other is inserted into a receptacle in the oven wall. When the selected temperature is reached, the oven signals and shuts off automatically. Control panels on some ovens display the temperature as it rises; some ovens switch to a low, holding setting instead of shutting off altogether when the selected temperature is reached.

Whole Meal Cooking Ovens with this feature may have a large interior and/or a metal shelf to allow cooking of more than one dish—or a whole meal, at one time. Foods must be carefully selected and placed, however, so that they take about the same cooking time and power.

Program Cooking   Some ovens contain preset cooking programs that adjust both time and power levels for specific cooking jobs. And on some, you can add your own programs—for favorite recipes or oft-repeated tasks.

These settings eliminate guesswork and the need of constantly referring to the cookbook. The systems vary in how they operate. Some ovens are preprogrammed for literally hundreds of cooking operations. The user simply enters basic data—such as type of food, doneness desired and weight—and the oven takes care of the rest. Even weight may sometimes be calculated automatically. Others involve using the temperature probe. Still others have an automatic humidity sensor, that responds to steam escaping from the food being cooked and then calculates the time and power needed to finish cooking the food properly.

Cookbook/Instruction Manual   This almost is as important a feature as any other; particularly with a new method of cooking. Before purchasing any microwave oven, check out these guides to see how complete and easy to use they are. Extensive recipes will be less important than clear, easy to find and follow, information on how to use the oven to full advantage and how to adapt favorite recipes—or portions of them—to microwave cooking.

[3]

Range-Top Cooking

Range-top cooking relies primarily on direct heat conduction from either a gas burner or electric heating element. Your choice of gas or electric fuel may depend on personal preference, the utility rates in your area, the fuel already provided to your home and the other appliances that you plan to use in the kitchen. Some cooks prefer the quick, instant response of gas cooking; others prefer the flameless control of electricity.

Once you have a microwave oven, you'll no doubt find you'll use it for functions you formerly used the range-top for—cooking vegetables and melting butter, for example. But the range-top always will be important:

• For quick sauteing or browning of meat or poultry.

• For large quantities of food.

• For the long, slow simmering needed to bring out full flavor in foods such as soups and sauces.

• For cooking pasta, rice, beans and other dried foods. While these can be cooked just as well in a microwave oven, there's no time savings, so you might as well reconstitute them on the range-top and save your microwave oven for other uses.

An electric grill-range will greatly expand the ease and pleasure of range-top cooking, making it possible to cook with an indoor grill and a variety of accessories such as griddle, wok or slow cooker in the most efficient manner possible.

Each of the topics that follow in this chapter gives specifics on the various types of range-top cooking, plus recipes most suitable for each.

CONVENTIONAL SURFACE UNITS

Since conventional range-top surface units rely primarily on conduction heating—direct transference of heat from one substance to another—the relation of the heat source and the cookware used on it is particularly important. Factors to be considered include the material, size and construction of each piece of cookware and the use of the proper heat setting.

The Cookware
Construction Optimum construction details of cookware are illustrated on the next page. You may not find all of them in any one line of cookware, and sometimes certain points are less important. In a large saucepan or stockpot, for example, an absolutely flat bottom (and excellent heat conduction) is less important than with a skillet. The water or other liquid in the saucepan helps produce even heating throughout (by convection), while the skillet relies almost totally on conduction heating.

Size The pan should fit the burner or element

Basic cookware

for more efficiency and safety. If a pan is larger than the element on an electric range, the porcelain enamel around the unit may become overheated, which can cause crazing or chipping of the enamel. If a pan is too small for an element or if gas flames are lapping around the sides of a pan, fuel is being wasted.

Materials   There is no one ideal cookware material—each has drawbacks as well as advantages. That's why you'll find so many choices of cookware on the market, and also find basic materials combined with each other, or with a special finish such as nonstick or porcelain enamel, in order to come closer to the "ideal" combination. You may want to choose different types of cookware for different purposes, or look for a set that most closely meets your criteria and cooking habits.

Aluminum comes in a wide range of styles, weights and prices. It conducts heat evenly and quickly; holds heat well. However, alkaline foods may darken it, salt can pit it, and custards and white sauces can take on a gray look. Lightweight, thin-gauge aluminum may warp and dent.

Stainless Steel is durable, attractive, easy to clean, doesn't react with food and resists stains. However, it is a poor conductor of heat, developing hot spots where foods can stick and burn. To overcome this problem, stainless steel is often wedded with another metal that conducts heat well, such as aluminum, copper or carbon steel.

Copper is an excellent heat conductor, but discolors easily and needs constant polishing to maintain its appearance. Because it reacts chemically with foods, interior surface must be of another material—usually stainless steel.

Cast Iron heats slowly and may develop hot spots, but holds heat well. It is extremely durable, but also heavy. It also rusts easily unless kept well seasoned.

Glass-ceramic resists cracking due to rapid temperature changes and is well suited to microwave ovens as well as conventional use. However, it is a poor conductor of heat, conducting heat slowly and unevenly.

SURFACE UNIT RECIPES

HOT CHOCOLATE AND VARIATIONS

1 tablespoon unsweetened cocoa powder
2 tablespoons sugar
Dash salt
Hot milk
1/8 teaspoon vanilla extract

Combine cocoa, sugar and salt in cup. Stir in hot milk to fill cup. Add vanilla extract; stir until blended.

1 serving

VARIATIONS

Canadian Cocoa: Add ⅛ teaspoon maple extract.

Irish Mint Cocoa: Add ⅛ teaspoon mint and pepper-
mint extract.

Orange Cocoa Cappucino: Add ⅛ teaspoon orange
extract.

Swiss Mocha: Add ½ teaspoon instant coffee gran-
ules.

Viennese Cocoa: Add dash ground cinnamon and
dash ground nutmeg. Serve with cinnamon stick
stirrer.

QUICK CREAMED ONIONS

4 cups sweet Spanish onion wedges (about 2 me-
    dium onions)
½ cup water
¼ cup dairy sour cream
2 tablespoons mayonnaise
2 tablespoons chopped pimiento
½ teaspoon salt

Put onion wedges and water into 1½-quart
saucepan. Bring to boil. Cover and simmer about 10
minutes or until onion is tender, stirring occasionally. Drain. Combine sour cream, mayonnaise, pimiento and salt. Add to cooked onions; toss gently.

4 servings

APPLE-SKILLET SUPPER
(photo in color section)

1 pound bulk pork sausage
1 teaspoon dried thyme leaves, crushed
⅓ cup packed brown sugar
¼ cup cider vinegar
4 cups shredded cabbage
2 small Red or Golden Delicious apples, cored and
    sliced in 16 wedges

Break up sausage in large skillet. Sprinkle with thyme. Cook until meat is browned. Add brown sugar and vinegar; mix well. Add cabbage. Cover. Cook 2 to 3 minutes or just until cabbage is wilted. Stir in apple slices. Cook 2 minutes.

4 servings

SAVORY BRAISED BRUSSELS SPROUTS

2 cups fresh brussels sprouts
2 cups water
½ teaspoon salt
¼ cup butter or margarine
2 tablespoons seasoned dry bread crumbs
2 tablespoons grated Parmesan cheese

Wash and trim brussels sprouts. Cover sprouts with salted water in medium saucepan. Bring to boil; simmer covered 6 to 8 minutes or until tender. Drain.

Melt butter in small skillet. Pour 3 tablespoons melted butter over sprouts. Add bread crumbs to butter remaining in skillet; brown crumbs. Sprinkle crumbs and cheese over sprouts; toss gently.

4 servings

CREAMY BEEF SOUP

¼ cup butter
1¼ cups water
2 cups shredded potatoes
2 tablespoons chopped onion
1 tablespoon flour
3 cups milk
1 package (4 ounces) smoked sliced beef, cut in
     small pieces
1 teaspoon beef stock base
1 can (7 ounces) vacuum-pack whole kernel corn
1 teaspoon salt
¼ teaspoon celery seed
⅛ teaspoon pepper
1 cup dairy sour cream
Chopped parsley

Melt butter in saucepan. Add water, potatoes and
onion. Cover; bring to boil. Reduce heat and simmer 20 to 25 minutes or until potatoes are tender.
Stir in flour. Cook 1 minute. Add milk gradually,
stirring constantly. Stir in beef, beef stock base,
corn, salt, celery seed and pepper. Blend in sour
cream gently. Heat to serving temperature. Garnish
with parsley.

6 servings

SKILLET ONION-ZUCCHINI CASSEROLE

2 medium sweet Spanish onions
2 medium zucchini
¼ cup butter or margarine
1 can (10¾ ounces) condensed cream of mushroom
    soup
Dash pepper
½ cup toasted buttered fine soft bread crumbs

Peel onions. Slice onions and zucchini ¼ inch
thick. Melt butter in large skillet. Add onion and
zucchini slices; cook 5 minutes, stirring occasionally. Add undiluted soup and pepper; stir gently.
Simmer covered 5 minutes or until zucchini is tender. Top with crumbs before serving.

4 to 6 servings

GRILLING

The "outdoor" flavor of grilled foods, indoors, all
year round is possible with special grill-ranges or
cooktops. These down-draft, ducted, grill-ranges
capture smoke, grease and odors efficiently and
vent them outside.

The grilling is faster and cleaner than with an
outdoor grill. The radiant heat duplicates the action
of charcoal, by vaporizing droplets of meat juices as
they strike the permanent grill-rock cartridges below.

Grill-range

Special Note About Charcoal Grilling

It is commonly believed that charcoal is necessary to provide foods with that "outdoor" flavor. This, however, is not true. The flavor actually is produced as fat and meat juices drip from the meat onto a super-heated surface—such as burning charcoal or fiery-hot grill-rocks. It is the smoke that is created, rising and bathing the food, that produces the unique flavor.

Grill Accessory Design

The grill accessory consists of:

1. Grill Grates
2. Heat Source
3. Grill-Rocks
4. Permanent Grill Basin
5. Method of Grease Removal

While these may be designed and constructed in various ways, this illustrates one design.

Grilling Tips

To insure the best possible results when grilling, follow the guidelines listed below:

• Before using the grill for the first time, wash grill grates in hot, soapy water; rinse and dry.

• Precondition new grates by brushing with vegetable oil or spraying with a non-stick vegetable coating. This procedure should be repeated after cleaning in a dishwasher since the detergent removes seasoning.

• For easier clean-up, as well as preventing meats from sticking to grates until they are seasoned, spray grates, grill-rocks and grill basin with a non-stick vegetable coating.

• Preheat grill according to manufacturer's directions. Preheating improves the flavor and appearance of meats and quickly sears the meat to help retain the juices. It will help give food that "branded" look. The heating element should glow a bright cherry red.

• For best results, buy top grade meat. Meat that is at least ¾-inch will grill better than thinner cuts.

• Excessive amounts of fat should be trimmed from meats. Only a normal amount is necessary to produce the smoke needed for that smoked, "outdoor" flavor. Excessive fat can create cleaning and flare-up problems.

• Use tongs with long handles or a spatula for turning meats. Do not use a fork as the tines will pierce the meat, allowing juices to be lost.

GRILL RECIPES

GRILLED SIRLOIN STEAK WITH MUSHROOM SAUCE

1 beef sirloin steak (about 2½ pounds) cut 1 inch
    thick
Salt and pepper
½ cup ⅛-inch mushroom slices
Mushroom Sauce (see recipe)

Place steak on grill over heat source. Grill until one side is browned. Season, turn and finish cooking on other side. Season. Steak requires 16 to 17 minutes for rare, 17 to 18 minutes for medium, and 18 to 19 minutes for well done. Top with sauce.

4 to 6 servings

MUSHROOM SAUCE

2 tablespoons butter
1 cup sliced mushrooms
½ cup sliced green onions
¼ cup water
2 teaspoons cornstarch
¼ teaspoon salt
½ cup milk

Melt butter in skillet. Add mushrooms and onions;
cook, stirring occasionally, over medium heat
about 4 minutes or until tender. Combine water,
cornstarch and salt; add gradually to vegetables,
stirring constantly. Stir in milk. Cook over low
heat, stirring occasionally, 4 minutes.

1¼ cups sauce

MAPLE-MUSTARD-GLAZED SPARERIBS

4 pounds pork spareribs
½ teaspoon salt
¾ cup barbecue sauce
¾ cup catsup
2 tablespoons brown sugar
2 teaspoons dry mustard

Sprinkle spareribs with salt. For sauce, mix barbecue sauce, catsup, brown sugar and mustard.

If using an outdoor grill, make foil drip pan, and
arrange slow coals on both sides of pan. Place ribs
on grill; lower grill hood or cover with foil tent.

Grill ribs 40 minutes. Turn ribs over. Continue
to grill, brushing ribs frequently with half of sauce.
Turn ribs over and continue to grill 10 minutes,
brushing frequently with remaining sauce.

About 4 servings

WOK COOKING

The wok was the standard utensil for Oriental cooking long before our ancestors settled in North America. In China, energy conservation was important centuries before it became an issue here, and the wok lends itself to both rapid cooking and slow cooking, using a minimum of fuel in either case.

Shaped like a large bowl, with sloping sides, a wok can be used for pan-frying, simmering, deep-frying, braising, steaming and even popping corn. But perhaps the most typical use—for which it has no equal—is stir-frying, the method most characteristic of Chinese cooking. In this, the food (usually small pieces of meat and vegetables) is cooked rapidly, requiring intense heat and constant stirring or tossing. While a wok isn't a must for stir-frying, it certainly has the advantage. The high sloping sides make it possible to turn and toss foods with abandon, and to swoop already-cooked foods to rest on the sides as fresh ingredients are added. Because woks are made of thin metal, there is the rapid, high-heat transfer that is necessary to stir-fry cooking or searing. But the shape and material also makes possible more gentle cooking—steaming vegetables or simmering soups.

A wok must have even, all-around contact with its heat source for proper cooking results. Conventional woks can be adapted for use on many kitchen ranges through use of a metal ring accessory that holds the round bottom steady and positions the wok at a proper height above the heat source. Woks also are available as small appliances. A versatile adaptation is the wok accessory for grill-ranges. In these, a specially-shaped, concave plug-in heating element conforms to the shape of the wok to provide uniform heat—high, low or in between, as the type of cooking requires. The concave element also holds the wok steady while in use.

The wok itself is made of iron, cold rolled carbon steel or stainless steel. Like cast iron pans, iron woks usually require seasoning—heat treatment with a vegetable oil—before and during use to prevent foods from sticking. Stainless steel woks don't require seasoning but, like other stainless steel cooking utensils, they may heat unevenly. Some woks are covered with a hard non-stick finish. This finish not only reduces the amount of care required, it also makes it possible to minimize the amount of oil required during cooking for more nutritious, lower-calorie cooking.

Stir-fry meal

Wok and Accessories

These are typical parts of a wok, and some of the accessories that often accompany it:

1. Wok Large capacity, with rounded bottom and gently-sloping sides, for cooking either small or large quantities of food. Should have two large handles, of a non-conductive material to make it easy to grasp without pot holders and to maneuver the wok during cooking, or to carry the wok to the table for serving.

2. Cover Large, dome-shaped—to increase the capacity of the wok when steaming large quantities of food such as corn-on-the-cob or lobster.

3. Steaming Rack Sits in base of wok; positions vegetables and other foods above boiling water, for gentle, nutritious cooking.

4. Accessories (a) Bamboo rice paddles, chopsticks, a ladle, skimmer, spatulas or (b) tempura rack often come with a wok or can be purchased separately. All are handy tools, and many Oriental cooking aficionados insist the food "tastes better" when prepared with non-metallic cooking utensils.

Wok Cooking Tips
Stir-frying:

• Heat oil in wok on highest temperature setting about 2 minutes, or until the oil is hot but not sizzling or smoking. A plastic condiment bottle can be used to ring the wok with vegetable oil. Peanut oil is best for stir-frying because it can be heated to high temperatures without smoking and its bland taste does not overpower the flavor of foods.

• Cut ingredients into small, uniform pieces. This helps food cook more quickly and evenly. Cutting foods on the diagonal helps tenderize them and exposes more food surface to the heat during cooking. Because of the speed of stir-frying, all ingredients should be prepared before cooking actually starts.

• Stir and toss foods constantly over high heat so that all pieces come in contact with the hot wok. Don't be timid—if a few pieces tumble out of the wok, so what? The rapid, even cooking is more important. Use bamboo rice paddles, chopsticks, wooden spatulas or other non-metallic utensils to keep the food in action.

• Stir-frying recipes are quite flexible and can combine almost any vegetables and meat that are on hand. First, stir-fry meat or other ingredients

Wok and accessories

that take longest to cook. When almost done, remove them or push them onto the sides. Add more
oil, if necessary. When oil is hot, add vegetables or
other quick-cooking foods and stir-fry until crisp-
tender. Then return meat and other cooked ingredients to the wok; add a sauce, if desired; and cook
and stir until liquid boils. Serve at once—because
foods are cooked so quickly, they cool down quickly, too.

Steaming:

• Steaming retains color, flavor and juiciness of
foods. It is a nutritious way to cook food, since little
or no added fat is needed, and vitamin and mineral
loss is minimal. It can be used for foods from seafood to dessert and can be used to reheat leftovers
without drying them out.

• To steam, add 2 to 2½ cups of water to the wok.
Then position the steaming rack securely in the bottom—the rack should not touch the water. Cover
the wok and heat on high until the water boils.
Place the food directly on the rack or on a pan in the
rack, leaving space around the sides for the steam to
circulate.

WOK RECIPES

ORIENTAL BEEF STIR-FRY

1¼ pounds beef top round steak, cut 1 to 1¼ inches
   thick
1 small head Iceberg lettuce
1 tablespoon cornstarch

1 teaspoon sugar
¼ cup soy sauce
1 tablespoon sherry
4 tablespoons vegetable oil, divided
1 clove garlic, cut in half
2 slices fresh ginger root
1 large red onion, sliced
8 ounces (about 2 cups) small mushrooms
1 large tomato, cut in 12 wedges

Partially freeze steak to firm. Slice steak diagonally across grain into very thin strips. Put into dish.

Core, rinse and thoroughly drain lettuce. To shred, halve head lengthwise, place halves cut-side-down and slice crosswise with stainless steel knife. Refrigerate shredded lettuce in plastic bag to crisp.

Combine cornstarch, sugar, soy sauce and sherry. Pour over steak strips, stirring to coat.

Heat 2 tablespoons oil in large skillet or wok until hot. Add garlic and ginger root and cook 5 seconds, stirring constantly; discard. Cook onion 3 minutes, stirring frequently. Add mushrooms and cook 2 minutes. Remove and keep warm. Drain marinade from steak strips; reserve. Quickly brown steak strips in remaining 2 tablespoons oil, stirring constantly. Add marinade and heat through. Stir in onion, mushrooms and tomato; heat thoroughly. Arrange lettuce on large platter. Serve beef stir-fry over lettuce.

5 or 6 servings

HUNGARIAN-STYLE FRESH FRY

2 tablespoons vegetable oil
2 cups (about ½ bunch) fresh broccoli flowerettes
½ cup sliced celery
2 cups shredded cabbage
½ pound fresh mushrooms, cleaned and sliced
2 cups cooked meat strips (3 × ⅜ inch)*
¼ cup gravy
¼ cup water
2 teaspoons paprika
1 teaspoon salt
¼ teaspoon caraway seed
⅛ teaspoon pepper
½ cup dairy sour cream
Mashed fresh potatoes, if desired

Heat oil in large skillet over medium-high heat. Add broccoli and celery. Cook, stirring frequently, 2 to 3 minutes. Add cabbage and mushrooms. Cook, stirring frequently, 2 to 3 minutes or until vegetables are crisp-tender. Remove vegetables to large bowl. Combine meat, gravy, water, paprika, salt, caraway seed and pepper in same skillet. Stir over medium heat until mixture is thoroughly heated. Return vegetables to skillet; toss lightly. Stir in sour cream. Heat thoroughly; do not boil. Serve with potatoes, if desired.

4 servings

* *Use any cooked meat such as beef pot roast, pork, ham, turkey or chicken.*

GRIDDLE COOKING

Somehow, a round frying pan just never quite suits the foods you most often cook in it. The bacon extends over the edges; there's not enough space for more than a few pancakes or eggs at one time; the food just "sits" in the extra fat that often accumulates, making foods soggy and adding extra calories.

The flat shape and grease drain are only a few advantages of a griddle. It can be an accessory to a modular grill-range. It may be designed to fit over the elements of a conventional gas or electric range or it can be a small appliance.

SLOW COOKING

Long, slow cooking of foods accomplishes several purposes: It brings out the full flavor of ingredients; it allows usage of fresh foods that might otherwise be discarded, and it provides a way to toss ingredients in a pot for a meal that might not be eaten until hours later.

Slow cooking of food can be done on any range by using a pot that conducts heat uniformly, at a slow, even temperature. Heavy-weight aluminum or cast iron pots, with close-fitting lids are the best choice cookware materials. Slow cookers, small appliances that plug into any conventional kitchen electrical outlet, were designed for this purpose. You also can use a deep cooker accessory available as an option on some grill-ranges.

SLOW COOKER RECIPES

LAMB STEW

2 pounds lean lamb shoulder or leg, cut in 1-inch
  cubes
1½ teaspoons salt
½ teaspoon dried thyme leaves, crushed
1 clove garlic, minced
1 onion, diced
½ cup sliced celery
4 large carrots, pared and cut in strips
1 can (16 ounces) tomatoes, cut in pieces
  (undrained)
1 pound potatoes, pared and cut in quarters
¼ cup cornstarch
½ cup water
1 package (10 ounces) frozen peas

Combine lamb, salt, thyme, garlic, onion, celery,
carrots, tomatoes and potatoes in Slow Cooker. Cover and cook on Low 8 to 10 hours. Dissolve cornstarch in water. Stir frozen peas and dissolved cornstarch into stew in Slow Cooker. Cover and cook on
High 1 hour or until stew is thickened.

6 servings

MANHATTAN-STYLE CLAM CHOWDER
(photo in color section)

1 cup chopped pared potatoes
1⅔ cups water
2 cans (16 ounces each) tomatoes, chopped
1 cup chopped celery
⅔ cup chopped green pepper
1 package (9 ounces) frozen cut green beans, thawed
1 tablespoon butter
1½ cups clam juice
¼ cup bacon bits
2 tablespoons catsup
1 tablespoon Worcestershire sauce
1½ teaspoons Italian seasoning
½ teaspoon dried basil leaves, crushed
¼ teaspoon thyme leaves, crushed
Salt and pepper to taste
2 bay leaves
1 cup or 16 cherrystone clams, shucked, drained
    and finely chopped

Cook potatoes 10 minutes in water in covered Dutch oven. Stir in tomatoes, celery, green pepper, green beans, butter, clam juice, bacon, catsup and seasonings. Simmer covered 45 minutes. Add clams. Simmer uncovered 2 to 3 minutes. Serve hot.

6 to 8 servings

[4]

Oven Cooking

Will the microwave oven and other newer kitchen cooking appliances replace your conventional oven? It's doubtful. There are a number of cooking functions at which a regular oven—be it gas or electric, radiant or convection—can't be beat:

Slow, Even Cooking It's essential for steam-leavened foods such as popovers. And even though a family favorite such as a meatloaf may cook just as well in the microwave oven, it may be preferable to put it in a regular oven and forget about it for an hour while preparing the rest of the meal.

Capacity Microwave ovens cook many things extremely well, and some are designed to cook several dishes at once. Even the largest microwave oven is usually only one-third the size of a conventional oven, and most cooks use the microwave oven for only one dish at a time. A conventional oven will handle larger quantities of food, and the slower cooking gives more flexibility to cooking times. And a convection oven, because of the forced, circulating air, makes it possible to place more food in less space than a conventional radiant oven, and have it cooked uniformly and well, without the "tending" (turning and stirring) often necessary in a microwave.

Browning The slow, dry, evaporative heat of conventional ovens produces the traditional brownness of roasts and of foods such as cookies, pie crusts and breads.

CONVENTIONAL OVENS

There are two choices of heat source in conventional ovens: gas or electric. As with cooktops (Chapter 3), the choice of fuel may depend on personal preference, local utility rates, the fuel already provided to the home and the other appliances in use in the kitchen.

(For design and features of gas and electric ovens, see Chapter 2.)

Three basic types of cooking are done in conventional ovens: baking, roasting and broiling. Here are the principles for best results with each process:

Oven Baking

Baking is a combination of two types of heat transfer—convection and radiation.

Convection is a rapid process of heat transfer that involves the movement of the heated matter itself from one place to another.

The oven air is heated by an electric element or gas burner in the bottom. As this air is heated, it expands and rises to the top, forcing the cooler, heavier air to go to the bottom to be heated. Approximately 30-40 percent of the heat in the oven is convected heat.

Radiation is the transfer of heat from one object to another without necessarily warming the matter in between. The heat can be felt almost instantly because it is traveling at the speed of light. For example, when you stand in the sun on a chilly day the sun warms you, but the air around you remains cool.

In oven baking, approximately 60-70 percent of the heat is radiant. When the bottom and sides of the oven become hot as it is heated, they radiate heat to the utensils and foods in the oven.

Oven Baking Tips

• Glass, metal or heat-proof containers can be used. The type of utensil finish determines the amount of browning that will occur. Dark, rough or dull utensils absorb heat resulting in a browner, crispier crust. Use this type for pies. Shiny or smooth utensils reflect heat, resulting in a lighter, more delicate browning. Cakes and sugar cookies require this type of utensil. Glass utensils also absorb heat. When baking in glass utensils, lower the recommended temperature by 25° F and use the recommended cooking time in the recipe. This is not necessary when baking pies or casseroles.

• For even cooking and proper browning, there must be adequate room for air circulation in the oven. Allow two inches between pans and from the oven walls. When baking on two racks, stagger the utensils so one is not directly above the other.

Oven baking

Never cover a rack entirely with a large cookie sheet or aluminum foil.

• Preheating is necessary for good results when baking breads, cookies and biscuits. For casseroles and roasts preheating is not necessary. To preheat, set the oven at the correct temperature—selecting a higher temperature doesn't shorten preheating time. For ovens without an indicator light allow ten minutes for preheating.

• Leave the oven door closed until the minimum baking time has elapsed. Opening the oven door frequently during cooking allows excessive heat to escape which wastes fuel and can affect baking results.

CONVENTIONAL OVEN RECIPES

CRANBERRY CHICKEN AND STUFFING (photo in color section)

1 broiler-fryer chicken (about 3 pounds), quartered
4 tablespoons butter or margarine, divided

1 package (1.5 ounces) dry onion soup mix, divided
1 can (16 ounces) whole cranberry sauce, divided
1½ cups hot water
1 package (6 ounces) top-of-stove stuffing mix, cornbread flavor
½ teaspoon celery salt
⅛ teaspoon pepper
¼ cup sliced unblanched almonds

Preheat oven to 350°. Place chicken quarters in 3-quart baking dish. On pieces of foil large enough to cover dish, rub 1 tablespoon butter and sprinkle half package soup mix. Rub chicken with 1 tablespoon butter and sprinkle with remaining half package soup mix. Drain liquid from cranberry sauce and drizzle over chicken. Reserve 1 cup cranberry sauce. Spread remaining cranberry sauce over chicken. Cover carefully with prepared foil.

Bake at 350° 40 minutes.

Mix hot water, vegetable-seasoning packet from stuffing, and remaining 2 tablespoons butter; stir until butter melts. Stir in cornbread stuffing crumbs until moistened. Mix in reserved cranberry sauce.

Remove foil from dish. Push chicken aside and add stuffing in 4 mounds. Drizzle pan drippings over stuffing. Sprinkle chicken with celery salt, pepper and almonds. Continue baking uncovered 20 minutes or until fork can easily be inserted in chicken. Drain off fat. Serve chicken with stuffing.

4 servings

HOLIDAY CHOCOLATE CAKE
(photo in color section)

2 cups sugar
1¾ cups all-purpose flour
¾ cup unsweetened cocoa powder
2 teaspoons baking soda
1 teaspoon baking powder
1 teaspoon salt
2 eggs
1 cup buttermilk
1 cup strong black coffee
½ cup vegetable oil
2 teaspoons vanilla extract
Ricotta Cheese Filling (see recipe)
Chocolate Whipped Cream Frosting (see recipe)
Vanilla Whipped Cream (see recipe)
Candied or maraschino cherries, if desired

Grease two 9-inch round layer cake pans. Line bottom of pans with wax paper circles. Grease and flour bottom and sides of pans. Preheat oven to 350°. Combine sugar, flour, cocoa, baking soda, baking powder and salt in large mixer bowl. Add eggs, buttermilk, coffee, oil and vanilla extract. Beat at low speed of electric mixer 30 seconds. Increase speed to medium and beat 2 minutes, scraping down sides occasionally (batter will be thin). Divide batter in prepared pans.

Bake at 350° 30 to 35 minutes or until cake tester inserted in center comes out clean. Cool 15 minutes. Remove cake layers from pans and peel off paper. Cool completely on racks.

To assemble cake, slice cooled cake layers in half horizontally. Place bottom slice on serving plate. Spread ⅓ of filling over cake. Alternate cake layers and filling, ending with cake. Frost cake with Chocolate Whipped Cream. Using pastry bag and tube, pipe Vanilla Whipped Cream on top. Decorate with cherries, if desired.

12 servings

RICOTTA CHEESE FILLING

1 container (15 ounces) ricotta cheese
¼ cup sugar
3 tablespoons orange-flavored liqueur
¼ cup candied red or green cherries, coarsely
    chopped
⅓ cup semisweet chocolate Mini Chips

Combine ricotta cheese, sugar and liqueur in bowl. Beat until smooth. Mix in cherries and chocolate.

Chocolate Whipped Cream: Combine ½ cup confectioners' sugar and 3 tablespoons unsweetened cocoa powder in small mixer bowl. Add 1½ cups whipping cream and 1½ teaspoons vanilla extract. Beat until stiff peaks form.

Vanilla Whipped Cream: Combine ½ cup whipping cream, 2 tablespoons confectioners' sugar and ½ teaspoon vanilla extract in small mixer bowl. Beat until stiff peaks form.

Oven Roasting
Roasting is the cooking of large tender cuts of meat uncovered and without adding moisture. Like oven baking, it utilizes both convection and radiant heat.

Oven Roasting Tips

• Use tender cuts of meat weighing three pounds or more. Some good choices are: beef rib, rib eye, top round, high quality tip and rump roasts, pork leg and loin roasts, veal and lamb leg, shoulder roasts and cured and smoked hams.

• Place meat fat side up on a rack in a shallow roasting pan. The rack holds the meat out of the drippings, allowing better heat circulation for even cooking.

• Most meats are roasted at 325° F. It is not necessary to preheat the oven. Place the roasting pan on a rack that has been placed in either of the two lowest rack positions.

• For more accurate results, use a meat thermometer. Insert the thermometer so the tip is in the center of the thickest part of the meat and not touching fat or bone.

• The internal temperature of a roast will rise approximately 5° F after it is removed from the oven —this is called residual cooking. Therefore, remove the roast from the oven when the thermometer registers approximately 5° F below the doneness wanted.

• Let the meat stand 15-20 minutes before serving. This allows the meat to reabsorb internal juices and makes carving easier.

Oven Broiling

Broiling is a dry heat cooking method used for tender steaks, chops and fish. It is accomplished by direct, radiant heat. In most ovens, only one side of the food at a time is exposed to the heat source.

Oven Broiling Tips

• Use the broiler pan supplied by the manufacturer. Most are two piece—the food is placed on the insert or top piece with holes so the fat drains into the solid bottom pan.

• Do not cover the insert with foil unless slits are made to allow the fat to drain. If the fat does not drain, it could start smoking and if left long enough could ignite.

• For easier clean-up the broiler pan (bottom piece) may be lined with foil.

• Meat for broiling should be at least one inch thick. This insures that the surface is not over-browned before the meat is completely cooked. To prevent the meat from curling, slash the edges.

• To prevent excessive spattering and smoking, trim fat from the meat. Adjust the distance of the meat from the heat source to achieve the degree of doneness wanted.

• Broiling times will vary according to several factors: the temperature and thickness of the meat, the distance of the meat from the heat source and the doneness wanted.

• Preheating the broiling area is not necessary unless darker browning is wanted. Do not preheat the broiler pan as this will cause the food to stick.

• When broiling in an electric range, the door

should be opened slightly. When using a gas range, usually this is not necessary.

• Use tongs instead of a fork to turn the meat. A fork pierces the meat and allows juices to escape.

CONVECTION OVENS

In convection cooking, a fan continuously circulates the heated air in the oven cavity while foods are cooking. In either a convection or radiant oven, the cooking process depends on the gradual conduction of heat from the outside of the food to the center. In a radiant (conventional) oven, the air is almost static. But in a convection oven, the power-driven heated air speeds up the cooking process. To illustrate, the layer of cold air always surrounding the food (since it is cooler than the oven it is in) is stripped away by the circulated heated air, speeding the conduction of heat into the food.

Convection cooking is not a new principle. In Europe, convection ovens have been standard equipment for commercial as well as residential use for years. Commerical bakeries and restaurants have been using convection ovens in the United States for more than 30 years. But the convection oven is just now beginning to come into its own for home use. (For a detailed description of convection ovens available, the features they offer and how they work, see Chapter 2.) To learn how to use a convection oven to best advantage, read these tips and the recipes that follow.

Convection baking

Convection Baking Tips

Foods   Convection cooking provides particularly good results with certain foods. There is a time-saving advantage when roasting meat or poultry. Breads, pastries, cookies and cakes come out crusty and golden brown from the convection oven.

Covered casseroles and Dutch ovens or those foods cooked in deep dishes do not benefit from convection cooking since the cover and high sides prevent the circulating air from reaching the food. However, foods will cook in these utensils and can be used in convection oven meals.

Temperature   For baked goods that require rising and browning, reduce the temperature by 25° F. Baking times should be about the same or slightly less. For other recipes, select the recommended temperature but reduce the time slightly.

Utensils Glass, metal or other heat-proof containers can be used. Products baked in dull, dark enamel or glass utensils tend to be more brown and crusty next to the pan surface because of the rapid heat absorption of the utensils. Shiny metal pans produce a light golden crust.

High-sided pans or covered dishes prevent circulating air from reaching the food and thus reduce time savings. Select cookie sheets without sides for convection baking. These allow circulating air to reach foods most effectively. A jelly roll pan (that has sides) can be inverted and used as a cookie sheet.

CONVECTION OVEN RECIPES

POPPY SEED BREAD
(photo in color section)

¼ cup poppy seed
Water
¼ cup instant minced onion
1 teaspoon instant minced garlic
2 packages active dry yeast
5½ cups (about) all-purpose flour, divided
2 cups rye flour
¼ cup sugar
1 tablespoon salt
2 eggs, divided
3 tablespoons shortening

Combine poppy seed with 1 cup water; set aside
45 minutes to soften. Drain; set poppy seed aside.
Combine onion and garlic with ¼ cup water; set
aside 10 minutes to soften. Dissolve yeast in 2
cups warm water (105 to 115°); set aside 5 minutes. Add 3 cups of all-purpose flour, rye flour,
sugar, salt, 1 egg and reserved poppy seed and
onion and garlic; beat until smooth, about 2 minutes. Add shortening; beat until smooth, about 2
minutes. Stir in enough of all-purpose flour (about
3 cups) to make soft dough.

Turn dough onto floured surface; knead in remaining flour. Knead until smooth and elastic,
about 10 minutes. Place in lightly greased bowl;
turn dough to bring greased surface to top. Cover
lightly; let rise in warm place until doubled in
bulk, about 1 hour. Punch down dough. Turn out
onto lightly floured surface. Divide dough into 3
equal pieces. Cover; set aside 10 minutes. With
floured rolling pin, roll out each piece into 12x8-
inch rectangle. Starting from narrow end, roll up
dough jelly-roll fashion. Place seam-side-down on
lightly greased baking sheets. Tuck ends under
and shape roll gently upward with hands to add
height. Cover; let rise in warm place until doubled
in bulk, about 45 minutes.

Preheat convection oven to 325°. With sharp
knife, slash top of each loaf on diagonal four times.
Combine remaining egg and 1 teaspoon water;
beat lightly. Brush evenly over loaves. Bake 25 to
30 minutes or until browned and bread sounds hollow when lightly tapped. Cool on racks.

3 loaves bread

SPICED CRANBERRY NUT BREAD
(photo in color section)

1½ cups chopped cranberries
1½ cups sugar, divided
3 cups all-purpose flour
2¼ teaspoons baking powder
2¼ teaspoons ground cinnamon
2 teaspoons grated orange peel
1½ teaspoons salt
¾ teaspoon baking soda
¼ teaspoon ground cloves
½ cup vegetable shortening
1 cup orange juice
2 eggs, beaten
1½ cups chopped walnuts

Preheat convection oven to 325°. Grease two
8½ × 4½ × 2-inch loaf pans. Combine cranberries
with ¼ cup sugar. Set aside. Combine flour, baking powder, cinnamon, orange peel, salt, baking
soda, cloves and remaining 1¼ cups sugar in large
bowl. Cut in shortening with pastry blender or
two knives until mixture resembles cornmeal.
Add orange juice and eggs; mix well. Stir reserved
cranberries into batter along with walnuts. Divide
equally in pans and spread evenly.

Bake at 325° about 45 minutes or until cake tester
inserted in center of bread comes out clean. Cool
10 minutes in pans on rack. Remove from pans
and cool on rack.

2 loaves bread

[5]

Microwave Cooking

If there's not a microwave oven in your
kitchen now, chances are there will be
in the near future.

For a complete description of the types of microwave ovens, their features and how they work, see
Chapter 2, pp. 29–43. For ideas on where to locate a
microwave oven, see Chapter 9, pp. 154–158.

If you're already an old hand at microwave cooking, you may want to skip right to the recipe ideas in
this chapter. If your microwave oven is relatively
new, or if you're still in the thinking stages and
don't own one yet, the following information provides some idea of what these ovens can do and how
they do it.

TECHNIQUES OF MICROWAVE COOKING

These techniques are not unique to microwave
cooking—they apply to conventional methods of
cooking as well. However, because of the speed of
microwave cooking, these principles are more ex-
aggerated.

Arrangement

When microwaving several items like cups of coffee, cupcakes or potatoes, arrange them in a circle around the center of the oven. Leave about two inches between each item so the microwaves can penetrate all sides of the food. The ideal shape for food placement is a donut or ring shape.

Arrange evenly shaped items, such as meatballs, in a circle in a round dish, leaving the center empty.

When cooking unevenly shaped foods such as fish filets or chicken pieces, arrange them so the larger or thicker portions are to the outside of the dish and the smaller or thinner portions are to the center. This arrangement enables more microwave energy to penetrate the larger portions for more even cooking of all the pieces.

Ring-shaped arrangement

"Critical" foods, those that attract more of the microwave energy such as cheese in sandwiches or meats in a stew, should be buried in the other ingredients to prevent overcooking. Arrange slices of cheese between slices of meat in a sandwich. For stews, soups, casseroles or pot roasts push the meat below the surface. Pieces of meat projecting above the surface will attract more microwave energy and will overcook.

Covering

Recipes usually indicate when and what type of covers should be used. The purpose of covering is to:

- Retain steam for more even and faster heating.
- Help tenderize tough meats or rehydrate dried lentils or beans.
- Keep foods moist—as when steaming fish.
- Prevent spattering of foods like bacon to reduce cleanup.

CAUTION: Steam quickly builds up during microwave cooking so use care when removing the cover to prevent steam burns.

Types of Covering Include:

Dish Lids will tightly cover food to help retain more moisture for faster cooking. This also will have a tenderizing effect.

Plastic Wrap can be used to form a tight seal for dishes that do not have their own lid. Turn back one corner of the wrap to form a vent to allow steam to escape. Use care when removing the plastic wrap to prevent steam burns.

Wax Paper will form a loose seal because it allows steam to escape. For example, use wax paper to wrap corn-on-the-cob for cooking or to line the bottom of a cake dish for easy removal of the cake after cooking. Wax paper also can be used to cover foods that tend to spatter. For bacon, however, paper towels are recommended.

Paper Towels can be used to loosely cover foods that spatter. Because paper towels absorb moisture, wrap sandwiches, breads or other baked goods in towels to prevent the food from becoming soggy.

Use paper towels to dry herbs or to refresh potato chips, pretzels or other snack foods. The towels will help draw moisture out and away from the food.

Steam fish and other seafood or soften foods such as tortillas in moistened paper towels.

Cooking or Roasting Bags Without Foil Ends can be used to cover food. Use a piece of string or cut a small strip from the opening of the bag as a tie if a plastic fastener is not provided.

Always follow the manufacturer's directions when using cooking bags in the microwave oven.

Aluminum Foil can be used to cover such foods as roasts, turkey or potatoes after cooking to prevent the surface of the food from cooling during the standing period. See **Shielding** for additional uses.

Shielding
Shielding is the use of aluminum foil to cover areas of food, especially unevenly shaped foods such as chicken, that begin to show signs of overcooking. Since microwave energy is reflected by metal (alu-

Shielding

minum foil), that portion of the food covered with foil will not absorb any more energy and thus cooking will be prevented. This principle also applies when defrosting foods in the microwave oven.

Pressure Release
Foods with thick skins, membranes or shells such as tomatoes, potatoes, chicken livers, egg yolks, eggs in the shell or squash will trap and hold steam during cooking. Eventually the food can no longer hold back the pressure and the food will burst. To prevent this, pierce or prick these foods before cooking to allow steam to escape. This also applies when using sealed freezer bags, cooking bags or boil-in-the-bags. Always cut a small opening in the bag to allow steam to escape.

Handling
Whether you are cooking a steak on the gas grill,

chocolate pudding on the surface unit, bacon in a conventional oven or a cake in the microwave oven, some attention (handling) will be necessary to insure even cooking results.

Because the microwave oven cooks so quickly, proper handling is particularly important.

Handling techniques include:

Stirring Scrambled eggs, soups, sauces or pudding. Because microwave energy penetrates all sides, stir from the outside in toward the center.

Turning the Dish Casseroles, meatloaf, cake, cookies or other foods that cannot be stirred.

Turning the Food Over Poultry, roasts, potatoes or other tall foods that tend to cook more near the top of the oven.

Rearranging the Food Chicken pieces, spareribs or fish fillets in a dish. Move the food from the center of the dish out to the edge of the dish.

Rearranging Dishes Several custard cups or individual serving dishes.

Pressure release

Variable Power Cooking

Early versions of microwave ovens offered just one
setting: Full Power. Just as the highest heat setting
is not always used with a range-top or conventional
oven, not all foods benefit from the full power output of a microwave oven. It simply cooks too quickly for some foods. Consequently, most microwave
ovens offer choices of power.

The choice of power levels varies from manufacturer to manufacturer. But basically it's the same
as selecting a heat setting on a surface unit. When
foods can tolerate or will benefit from rapid cooking, a higher power setting is selected; when gentler
cooking is needed, a lower power setting is selected. And, as is true with conventional cooking, the
microwave power setting can be changed during
the cooking process. Onions and green peppers for a
casserole, for example, might be sauteed at a high
power setting; the casserole cooked at a lower setting.

Standing Time and Carry-over Cooking

Standing time allows heat that builds up in the
outer layers to spread to the center to complete
cooking.

During this period some additional cooking will
take place—referred to as "carry-over cooking." For
this reason food should be removed from the oven
before it is completely cooked. Expect about a 10° F
rise in temperature during the standing period for
large foods such as a roast or chicken; less for smaller
or less dense foods. Cover foods cooked uncovered
with aluminum foil to prevent the surface from
cooling during the standing period.

Cover foods during standing time

FACTORS AFFECTING COOKING TIME

The following factors affect the cooking times of both conventional and microwave methods of cooking. However, they are more noticeable in microwave cooking because of the speed at which cooking takes place.

Starting Temperature

The colder the food, the longer it takes to cook. For example, refrigerated food will take a few minutes longer to cook than the same food at room temperature. Likewise, frozen foods will take longer than unfrozen foods, such as frozen peas versus canned.

Larger quantities increase cooking time

Quantity

As the quantity, volume, amount, size or thickness of the food increases, so does the cooking time. It does not matter whether it is one potato versus four potatoes or a small potato versus a large potato. When the quantity is increased, the cooking time will increase as well.

It is necessary to increase the cooking time as the quantity of food is increased because the oven is producing the same amount of energy at all times and focusing all the energy on whatever quantity of food is in the oven. Cooking time does not necessarily double if the amount of food is doubled.

Shape

The ideal shapes for microwave cooking are a round shape and a ring/donut shape since microwaves penetrate all sides of exposed foods. These shapes give the fastest, most even cooking results. Corners, by contrast, receive more energy because there are more exposed surfaces, thus, corners tend to overcook.

Shape affects cooking times and cooking results in several ways:

• Thin areas or thin foods cook faster than thick areas or thick foods. Since microwaves penetrate only to a depth of ¾ to 1½ inches, thicker foods are cooked by heat created by microwaves and by thermal conduction of that heat to the center of the food.

• Unevenly shaped foods are difficult to cook uniformly because of the unevenness of the food itself. To improve this situation, cover the thin areas with small pieces of aluminum foil to prevent overcooking.

• For faster cooking, avoid stacking food. It is better to spread food out over a larger area.

• Small, uniform shapes cook faster and more evenly than large, unevenly shaped foods. Keep this in mind when shaping meatballs, cutting stew beef or chopping vegetables for a casserole.

• Height also affects cooking times. When selecting hams, roasts or when shaping meatloaf, keep in mind that a low profile shape cooks more evenly. Since most microwave ovens have the energy source at the top, tall profile food will cook faster at the top where there is a higher concentration of energy.

Density
Although foods may be the same size, foods of different densities will cook at different rates of speed because the density of a food determines how mi-

crowaves will be absorbed. Foods such as a potato or roast will cook slower than a porous food such as cake because the depth of microwave penetration will not be as great with these foods.

Types of Food
Fatty or bony foods cook faster than meaty foods of the same weight. For example, fatty ground beef will cook faster than lean ground chuck. Liquid foods may heat faster than chunks of food in a mixture such as stew. Light, airy foods cook faster than heavy, thick or dense foods. Foods with high sugar or fat content will cook faster than foods with less sugar or fat.

Cooking Speed
The power setting selected and the oven wattage will affect cooking time.

High Altitude Cooking
Although high altitude adjustments made for conventional cooking usually are not required for microwave cooking, cooking times may increase slightly.

COOKWARE

While the choice of microwave cooking accessories was once somewhat limited more and more manufacturers have designed products specifically for use in microwave ovens, or for use in conventional and convection ovens as well. Food companies, too, have designed packaging for use in microwave as well as conventional oven or range-top cooking.

Check labeling on packaging or on the product itself to see if it is designed for microwave cooking. If in doubt, or to check cooking utensils you already own, see the "Utensil Test" in this section.

Note: Microwave energy will not heat any utensil that is safe for microwave oven use, since the microwaves simply pass through the utensil. A container may become hot, however, from heat or steam transferred from the food. In some cases, it may be necessary to use pot holders.

Cookware Materials

Glass Glass materials that are safe for microwave cooking include heatproof glass, ceramic, glass-ceramic, china and some pottery or earthenware.

Do Not Use fine china, lead crystal or any glass utensil trimmed or decorated with metal.

Paper Paper products that can be used in the microwave oven include paper plates, napkins, towels, cups and wax paper.

Do not use:

• Paper towels with nylon or other synthetic fibers—the paper could ignite.

• Foil-lined paper products—the foil will reflect microwaves and prevent or slow down cooking.

• Newspaper—some types of newpaper ink can absorb microwaves, causing the paper to ignite.

Plastics High-temperature plastics, dishwasher-safe plastics, styrofoam, plastic wraps, boil-in-the-bag plastics and roasting or cooking bags (without the wire twist tie) can all be used in the oven to some extent.

Don't use plastics, other than the thermo or high-temperature plastics, with foods high in fat or sugar. An example of high-temperature (polysulfone or thermo-set-filled polyester) plastic is bacon racks designed for use in the microwave oven. Foods high in fat or sugar become so hot that they can distort or even melt plastics such as styrofoam or plastic spoons.

There are many grades of plastic wrap. Some are heavy enough to withstand the high temperatures of cooking foods. Others will not withstand the high temperatures and will tear or even melt.

Melamine plastic utensils are not recommended for use in the microwave oven. They are made of a material that absorbs microwave energy and become hot.

Wood   Cutting boards, platters or utensils can

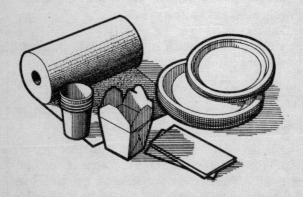

Microwave-safe paper products

Microwave oven cookware

be used for short-term heating only. Longer cooking will cause wood to dry out and warp or crack.

UTENSIL TEST

Most utensils made from glass, paper or plastic can be used in the microwave oven. To determine if a utensil is microwave safe, use this simple test:

Place utensil in the oven along with one cup of cool water (either next to or on the utensil).

Microwave for one minute on highest setting.

• If the utensil is **Hot**—it is Not Safe and should not be used in the oven.

• If the utensil is **Warm**—use the utensil for short-term heating only.

• If the utensil is **Cold** and the water is **Hot**—the utensil is safe for use in the microwave oven.

Metal Should not be used in the oven for the following reasons:

• If microwave energy comes in contact with metal, arcing (an electrical discharge causing a spark) and overheating of the metal may occur. This will damage the utensil and may cause damage to the oven cavity.

• If food is placed in a metal container, the metal will reflect microwaves away from the food. Cooking will not take place if the food is completely enclosed in metal, or will be slowed down or uneven if partially covered in metal.

• Exceptions: Some metal can be safely used if directions are carefully followed. For example:

• Aluminum foil can be used to shield or protect food from beginning to cook during a defrost operation or from overcooking during a cooking operation. The foil will reflect microwaves away from these sensitive areas, especially on uneven foods. Be sure foil does not come close to or touch oven walls or arcing will occur.

• Metal meat or candy thermometers designed for use in a microwave oven can be used. However, do not use conventional thermometers.

• Metal clamps (found on whole poultry holding the legs in place) and metal skewers (for Shish Kabobs) can be used. However, this metal should not be allowed to come in contact with the oven walls.

MICROWAVE OVEN RECIPES

GLAZED BOSC PEAR SUNDAES

3 fresh Bosc pears (about 1 ½ pounds)
¼ cup butter
½ cup apricot preserves
½ teaspoon vanilla extract
6 scoops vanilla ice cream

Halve and core pears. Arrange pear halves in 8-inch square glass baking dish with narrow ends toward center of dish. Dot with butter. Cover with plastic wrap. Cook in microwave oven 6½ to 7½ minutes at High, rotating dish one-quarter turn halfway through cooking time. Let stand 2 minutes. Put pear halves cut-side-up in serving dishes. Top with ice cream. Stir preserves and vanilla extract into butter in baking dish. Spoon sauce over ice cream and pears.

6 servings

SUPER SCRAMBLE

¼ pound bulk pork sausage
1 can (8¾ ounces) whole kernel golden corn, drained
¼ cup chopped green onion
6 eggs
⅓ cup milk
½ teaspoon salt
⅛ teaspoon pepper

Put double thickness of paper toweling on bottom of microwave-safe 9x9x2-inch baking dish. Crumble sausage onto paper toweling in dish. Cook in microwave oven *2½ to 3 minutes at High*. Slip out paper toweling. Stir in corn and onion, spreading evenly in dish. Cook in microwave oven *1 minute at High*.

Beat eggs, milk and seasonings with fork. Pour egg mixture over sausage mixture. Cover with plastic wrap. Cook in microwave oven *5 minutes at High*; stir after 3 minutes to move cooked portions from edges to center. Let stand covered 1 to 2 minutes before serving. (Remove scrambled eggs from oven when they are slightly underdone; heat retained in eggs completes cooking.)

4 servings

ONION STUFFED FISH ROLLS

2 tablespoons butter
1 medium sweet Spanish onion, chopped
½ pound fresh mushrooms, cleaned and chopped
¼ teaspoon salt
¼ teaspoon dried thyme leaves, crushed
4 or 5 white fish fillets (about 1½ pounds)
Salt and pepper
1 can (10¾ ounces) condensed cream of mushroom
   soup
⅓ cup dry white wine or milk
2 tablespoons chopped parsley

Melt butter in 1-quart glass measuring pitcher in microwave oven *30 to 40 seconds at High.* Stir in onion and mushrooms. Cook *4 to 5 minutes at High* or until tender. Season with ¼ teaspoon salt and thyme. Sprinkle fillets lightly with salt and pepper. Spoon onion mixture onto fillets. Roll each one up carefully; secure with picks. Place fish rolls in circle in 8-inch round glass cake dish.

Combine undiluted soup, wine and parsley. Spoon over fish. Cover with plastic wrap. Cook in microwave oven *10 to 12 minutes at High* or until fish is done, rotating every 5 minutes.

4 or 5 servings

STRAWBERRY OMELET

1 cup strawberries, washed and hulled
1 teaspoon sugar
4 eggs
¼ cup water
½ teaspoon salt
⅛ teaspoon pepper
2 tablespoons butter

Reserve 1 strawberry for garnish. Sprinkle remaining berries with sugar. Set aside.

Beat eggs slightly in bowl. Mix in water, salt and pepper thoroughly.

Melt butter in 9-inch glass pie plate in microwave oven *about 60 seconds at High*. Pour egg mixture into pie plate. Cover with plastic wrap. Cook 6 *to 7 minutes at Medium-High (80% power)* or until almost set. As edges of omelet begin to thicken, draw cooked portions toward center with spoon or fork to let uncooked mixture flow to bottom; tilt pie plate as necessary, but do not stir.

Remove from oven. Top with strawberries. Using pancake turner, fold omelet in half, turning out onto plate with quick flip of wrist. Top with reserved strawberry.

2 servings

BLUSHING RICE TOMATO CUPS
(photo in color section)

6 large firm ripe tomatoes
Salt and pepper
2 tablespoons butter or margarine
½ cup chopped onion
½ cup chopped green pepper
1 can (4 ounces) sliced mushrooms, drained
1 can (8 ounces) whole kernel golden corn, drained
3 cups cooked rice
1 teaspoon salt
¼ teaspoon pepper
½ cup diced Cheddar cheese, divided
Paprika

Wash tomatoes; cut slices from top of each tomato. Cut out center pulp and reserve. Sprinkle tomato shells with salt and pepper. Turn upside down to drain.

Melt butter in shallow 2-quart microwave-safe dish in microwave oven *1 to 1½ minutes at High.* Add onion and green pepper. Cook *1 to 2 minutes at High* or until crisp-tender. Stir in mushrooms, corn, rice, reserved tomato pulp, 1 teaspoon salt and ¼ teaspoon pepper. Cook *3 to 4 minutes at High.* Mix in ¼ cup cheese.

Spoon ½ cup mixture into each tomato shell. Top filled shells with remaining ¼ cup cheese. Sprinkle with paprika. Spread remaining filling in 2-quart glass baking dish. Place filled tomatoes on top of mixture in dish. Cook in microwave oven *6 to 7 minutes at High*, rotating dish ¼ turn after 3 minutes. Let stand 2 to 3 minutes.

6 servings

[6]

Complementary Cooking

Only a generation ago, most people prepared all foods using a conventional gas or electric range as the sole cooking appliance. How things have changed! Not only has the efficiency of conventional ranges been improved, but new cooking methods—such as convection ovens, microwave ovens and indoor grill-ranges and cooktops have become increasingly popular.

With all these cooking methods available, it can seem a bit overwhelming to know which appliance to use for what purpose. The secret is not to be overwhelmed, but to put each new appliance or technology to its best use.

The concept of "best use" isn't really new—even before gas stoves and electric ranges were invented, cooks had to learn how to build and bank a fire for proper baking, roasting or simmering; determine which sequence to cook foods in so that everything would be done at once; figure out how to keep

foods warm or reheat them without overcooking. Current appliance technology has made these and many other cooking tasks easier and much more foolproof, plus producing results that just weren't available before.

So, which of today's appliances to use for what? While each appliance excels at certain jobs and provides adequate to good results on others, no one appliance is ideal for preparing all foods. The key to success is to mesh their use for the combination that will result in a good-tasting, nutritious dish or meal most efficiently and easily.

Chapters 3, 4 and 5 explain the advantages of the various cooking methods available today, including recipes designed to show what each appliance does best. Now it's time to pull them together, with "Complementary Cooking," a common sense approach to determine which appliance or appliances to use to get the best results.

For a cream pie, for example, the crust can be cooked in either a conventional or microwave oven; the filling prepared on a range-top or in the microwave; and a meringue topping browned in the conventional oven.

You've probably been using complementary cooking with conventional appliances without thinking much about it. The following chart will help expand the concept and incorporate a microwave oven as part of complementary cooking.

The guide lists 60 common foods in thirteen categories, from appetizers to desserts. It shows at a glance which cooking appliance is best used to prepare the food—microwave oven, conventional oven or range-top, plus helpful tips for each food.

When more than one cooking method is satisfactory, that is indicated, along with the preferred cooking method. And it indicates when using a combination of cooking appliances will save time or produce a better product. This trading back and forth is what is meant by "Complementary Cooking"—using appliances together to "complement" each other.

To take the complementary cooking concept even farther, the recipes following the chart are designed to combine the best features of at least two major cooking appliances. They serve two purposes: Each recipe is not only excellent on its own, but will give ideas on how to adapt family favorites to make them even easier or better by utilizing new appliance concepts.

COMPLEMENTARY COOKING GUIDE

Food Category	Cooking Method				Complementary Cooking Tips
	Range-Top	Conventional Oven	Microwave Oven	Convection Oven	
Appetizers					
Bacon-wrapped Tidbits	No	Yes	*	Yes	There is a time advantage when cooking up to 4–6 servings in a microwave oven.
Hot Dips (cheese, meat, seafood, etc.)	Yes	Yes	*	Yes	There is a time advantage when cooking up to 4–6 servings in a microwave oven.
Spreads, Pates, Terrines	Yes	Yes	Yes	Yes	There is a time advantage when cooking up to 2 cups of spreads in a microwave oven. If pastry-covered bake in conventional or convection oven.

Key

*–Maytag's Preferred Method   C–Complementary Cooking

COMPLEMENTARY COOKING GUIDE continued

Food Category	Range-Top	Cooking Method			Complementary Cooking Tips
		Conventional Oven	Microwave Oven	Convection Oven	
Stuffed Vegetables (mushrooms, green peppers, artichoke bottoms, etc.)	C	Yes, C	Yes, C	Yes, C	There is a time advantage to cooking up to 4–6 servings in a microwave oven. Stuffing may be cooked on surface unit.
Beverages					
Milk-based (cocoa)	Yes	No	*	No	Up to 3 individual cups may be heated or reheated efficiently in microwave oven.
Water-based (coffee, tea, cider or wine)	Yes	No	*	No	Up to 3 individual cups may be heated or reheated efficiently in microwave oven.
Soups					
Vegetable-meat	Yes	No	*	No	Less stirring and time required when cooking up to 2 cups in microwave oven.

Cream	Yes	No	*	No	Less stirring and time required when cooking up to 2 cups in microwave oven.
Dried Bean, Pea	*	No	No	No	Requires long, slow cooking time. Best prepared on range-top.
Canned, Frozen	Yes	No	*	No	There is a time advantage when heating up to 2 cups in microwave oven. May be heated in serving bowl.
Dehydrated	Yes	No	*	No	Up to 2 cups may be heated in microwave oven.
Sauces					
Cream or Cheese	Yes	No	*	No	There is a time advantage when cooking up to 2 cups in microwave oven. May cook in serving bowl.

Key
*—Maytag's Preferred Method   C—Complementary Cooking

COMPLEMENTARY COOKING GUIDE continued

Food Category	Cooking Method			Complementary Cooking Tips
	Range-Top	Conventional Oven	Microwave Oven	Convection Oven	
Gravy	Yes	No	Yes	No	There is a time advantage when cooking up to 2 cups in microwave oven. May cook in serving bowl.
Hollandaise	Yes	No	*	No	Less stirring required when cooking up to 1½ cups in microwave oven.
Spaghetti	*	No	Yes	No	Time advantage when cooking up to 2 cups in microwave oven. Develop flavors with long, slow conventional cooking.

					Comments
Pasta, Rice	*	No	Yes	No	For best results, prepare on surface unit. Little or no time saving in microwave oven.
Meats & Poultry					
Roast—Tender (beef rib or sirloin, pork, leg of lamb, veal sirloin)	No	*	Yes	*	Up to 3—4 pounds may be microwaved.
Roast—Less Tender (chuck, rump, arm, etc.)	Yes	Yes	Yes	Yes	Up to 3—4 pounds may be microwaved.
Steaks, Chops, Kabobs—Tender (beef, T-bone, pork shoulder, rib, lamb, veal)	Yes	Yes	Yes	Yes	Up to 4 servings may be prepared in microwave oven using browning pan.
Steaks—Less Tender (round, chuck, etc.)	Yes	Yes	Yes	Yes	Up to 3—4 pounds may be tenderized, then microwaved.
Meatloaf	No	No	Yes	Yes	There is a time advantage when cooking a meatloaf in the microwave oven.

Key

*—Maytag's Preferred Method   C—Complementary Cooking

COMPLEMENTARY COOKING GUIDE continued

Food Category	Cooking Method				Complementary Cooking Tips
	Range-Top	Conventional Oven	Microwave Oven	Convection Oven	
Hamburgers	Yes	Yes	Yes	Yes	Up to 4–6 burgers may be microwaved using browning pan.
Stew Meat, Meatballs	Yes	Yes	Yes	Yes	Up to 4–6 servings may be microwaved. Use range-top or oven for larger amounts.
Fully-cooked boneless ham	No	Yes	Yes	Yes	Up to 3–4 pounds may be microwaved.
Uncooked large bone-in ham	Yes	Yes	No	*	Do not prepare uncooked bone-in ham in microwave oven.
Spareribs	Yes, C	Yes, C	Yes, C	Yes, C	Up to 4 servings (also sauces) may be microwaved. Sauces also may be prepared on surface unit.

Whole Bird (chicken, turkey, duck, capon, goose, etc.)	Yes	Yes	Yes	Yes	There is a time advantage when defrosting and cooking a bird up to 13 pounds in the microwave oven. For larger birds there is a time advantage by cooking it in a convection oven.
Cut-up Chicken (halves, quarters)	Yes, C	Yes	Yes, C	Yes	There is a time advantage when cooking up to 4–6 servings in a microwave oven. Pre-brown chicken on range-top.
Seafood Fish Fillets & Steaks	Yes	Yes	*	Yes	Quick, moist cooking is best for these delicate foods.

Key
*–Maytag's Preferred Method   C–Complementary Cooking

COMPLEMENTARY COOKING GUIDE continued

Food Category	Range-Top	Conventional Oven	Microwave Oven	Convection Oven	Complementary Cooking Tips
Whole Fish	Yes	Yes	Yes	Yes	A large fish may cause problems in microwave oven, under broiler or on range-top.
Shrimp	Yes	Yes	Yes	Yes	Up to 1 pound of shrimp may be microwaved.
Scallops	Yes	Yes	*	Yes	Up to 1 pound may be microwaved.
One-Dish Meals & Casseroles					
Meat, Poultry or Seafood	C	C	*, C	C	There is a time advantage when cooking up to 4 servings (also sauces) in microwave oven.

Macaroni and Cheese	Yes, C	C	Yes, C	C	There is a time advantage when cooking up to 4 servings (also sauces) in microwave oven. Cook macaroni on range-top.
Chili/Goulash	Yes	Yes	Yes	Yes	There is a time advantage when cooking up to 4 servings in a microwave oven.
Egg and Cheese Dishes					
Omelets	*, C	C	No	C	French omelets are best prepared on surface unit. Finish puffy omelets in conventional or convection oven.
Souffles	C	*, C	C	*, C	Base may be cooked in microwave oven or on range-top. Bake beaten egg mixtures in conventional or convection oven.
Scrambled	Yes	No	*	No	There is a time advantage when cooking 2–3 servings in microwave oven.

Key

*—Maytag's Preferred Method   C—Complementary Cooking

COMPLEMENTARY COOKING GUIDE continued

| | Cooking Method | | | |
Food Category	Range-Top	Conventional Oven	Microwave Oven	Convection Oven	Complementary Cooking Tips
Fried	*	No	Yes	No	Cook 2 or 3 at a time, pierce egg yolk and use browning pan when cooking in microwave oven.
Poached	Yes	No	Yes	No	Cook up to 2 at a time, pierce egg yolk and drop into hot water when cooking in microwave oven.
Fondue or Rarebit	Yes	No	*	No	There is less stirring and time required when cooking in microwave oven.
Quiche	No	*	Yes	*	Pie crust bakes best in conventional oven.

Melted Cheese Sandwiches	Yes	Yes	No	Yes	Toast bread: melt cheese in microwave oven or under broiler. Fry on surface unit.
Vegetables					
Fresh (peas, beans, carrots, spinach)	Yes	No	•	No	Up to 2 cups or 1 pound may be microwaved.
Potatoes, Winter Squash (baked)	No	No	Yes	Yes	Up to 4 potatoes or squash halves may be microwaved.
Potatoes, Winter Squash (boiled or mashed)	Yes	No	Yes	No	Up to 1 pound may be microwaved. Use range-top for larger amounts.
Sauced Vegetable Dishes (from scratch, i.e., scalloped potatoes)	C	Yes, C	Yes	Yes	Time advantage when cooking up to 4 servings in microwave oven. Sauce may be prepared in microwave oven or on range-top.

Key

* –Maytag's Preferred Method   C–Complementary Cooking

COMPLEMENTARY COOKING GUIDE *continued*

Food Category	Cooking Method				Complementary Cooking Tips
	Range-Top	Conventional Oven	Microwave Oven	Convection Oven	
Fruits					
Whole Fruits (baked/poached)	Yes	Yes	Yes	Yes	There is a time advantage when cooking up to 6 whole fruits in microwave oven.
Cut-up Fruits (dried & stewed)	Yes	Yes	Yes	Yes	There is a time advantage when cooking up to 2 cups in microwave oven.
Breads					
Quick Breads (loaves) i.e., Banana Nut Bread	No	*	Yes	*	Use special recipe for microwave oven.
Yeast Breads— Loaves, Dinner & Sweet Rolls	No	*	C	*	Microwave oven may be used to shorten rising time or for melting shortening.

Muffins, Biscuits	No	Yes	Yes	Yes	Use special muffin pans in microwave oven. Bake biscuits in convection or conventional oven.
Desserts Cakes (layer)	No	Yes	Yes	Yes	Packaged cake mixes may be microwaved. Cakes with beaten egg whites should be baked in conventional or convection oven.

Key

*—Maytag's Preferred Method   C—Complementary Cooking

BREADS AND BAKERY GOODS

HERBED WHOLE WHEAT SWIRL BREAD (photo in color section)

2 tablespoons instant minced onion
2 tablespoons water
½ cup butter or margarine
2 tablespoons dried parsley flakes
½ teaspoon dried marjoram leaves, crushed
½ teaspoon dried oregano leaves, crushed
½ teaspoon dried thyme leaves, crushed
4 cups all-purpose flour
2 cups whole wheat flour
2 packages active dry yeast
2 teaspoons salt
2 cups milk
2 tablespoons molasses
2 eggs

Combine onion and water. Set aside 10 minutes to soften.

Melt butter in 2-cup glass measuring cup in microwave oven *about 1 minute at High*. Add parsley, marjoram, oregano, thyme and reserved onion; set aside. Combine flours, yeast and salt. Put 2 cups of flour mixture into large bowl of electric mixer; set remaining flour mixture aside.

Put milk, molasses and ¼ cup reserved herb butter into 1-quart measuring pitcher. Heat in microwave oven *2 minutes at High* or until milk is scalded. Let cool to warm (about 120°). Add warm mixture to the 2 cups flour mixture. Beat at low speed of mixer until blended, about 1 minute. Beat at high speed 2 minutes. Reduce speed to low. Add 2 cups reserved flour mixture gradually, beating well. Beat in eggs, one at a time. Blend in remaining flour mixture, using wooden spoon if necessary. Turn dough out onto lightly floured surface. Knead until smooth and elastic, about 10 minutes. Place dough in well-greased bowl. Turn to bring greased surface to top. Cover; let rise in warm place until doubled in bulk, about 1 hour. Punch down dough. Divide into four equal pieces. Knead each piece on lightly floured surface until smooth. Cover pieces with towel. Set aside 10 minutes. Using floured rolling pin, roll each piece into 10x4 ½-inch rectangle. Spread 1 tablespoon reserved herb butter over each rectangle. Starting from narrow end, tightly roll up dough jelly-roll fashion. Place each loaf seam-side-down in greased 5½x3¼x2¼-inch loaf pan. Cover; let rise in warm place until doubled in bulk, about 1 hour.

Preheat oven to 350°. Brush remaining herb butter over loaves. Bake about 30 minutes or until golden brown and bread sounds hollow when lightly tapped. Turn out of pans; cool on racks.

4 loaves bread.

CORNBREAD

1 cup enriched yellow cornmeal
1 cup all-purpose flour
4 teaspoons baking powder
½ teaspoon salt
¼ cup vegetable shortening
1 cup milk
1 egg

Preheat oven to 425°. Combine cornmeal, flour, baking powder and salt in bowl. Melt shortening in 1-cup glass measuring cup in microwave oven *about 1 minute at High*. Stir milk, egg and melted shortening into cornmeal mixture. Beat until almost smooth. Turn batter into greased 8-inch square baking pan.

Bake at 425° 20 to 25 minutes or until wooden pick comes out clean when inserted in center.
One 8-inch square cornbread

BROCCOLI SPOON BREAD

1 small bunch broccoli
2 tablespoons water
⅛ teaspoon salt
¾ cup yellow cornmeal
2 tablespoons flour
1 teaspoon salt
2 cups water
4 tablespoons butter or margarine, divided
1 cup sliced celery
¼ cup chopped onion
4 eggs, separated
1 cup milk
1 cup shredded Cheddar cheese
¼ teaspoon liquid hot pepper sauce

Remove leaves and stems from broccoli. Separate broccoli into flowerettes (about 1½ cups). Put broccoli into 1-quart glass casserole. Combine 2 tablespoons water and ⅛ teaspoon salt. Pour over broccoli in casserole. Cover. Cook in microwave oven *2 minutes at High* or until just tender. Drain and set aside.

Combine cornmeal, flour and 1 teaspoon salt in 2-quart glass measuring pitcher. Add 2 cups water gradually, stirring until smooth. Cook in microwave oven *5 to 6 minutes at High* or until thickened; stir every 2 minutes. Stir in 2 tablespoons butter.

Preheat oven to 375°. Melt remaining 2 tablespoons butter in 1-quart glass casserole in microwave oven *30 seconds at High*. Stir in celery and onion. Cook *3 to 4 minutes at High* or until tender; stir once. Set aside. Beat egg yolks; blend into cornmeal mixture. Stir in milk, cheese, pepper sauce, cooked broccoli, celery and onion. Beat egg whites to stiff but not dry peaks; gently fold into cornmeal mixture. Turn mixture into buttered 2-quart glass casserole.

Bake at 375° 55 to 60 minutes or until top is crusty and golden brown.

About 6 servings

EGGS AND CHEESE

LEAF LETTUCE FRITTATA
(photo in color section)

4 cups (about 5 ounces) coarsely chopped leaf let-
    tuce
1 teaspoon water
3 tablespoons butter
½ cup chopped onion
8 eggs
¼ cup grated Parmesan cheese
1 teaspoon dried parsley flakes
1 teaspoon dried basil leaves, crushed
¼ teaspoon salt
¼ teaspoon dry mustard
⅛ teaspoon pepper

Preheat oven to 350°. Combine lettuce and water in
medium saucepan. Cook covered over medium
heat until soft, about 4 minutes. Drain well,
pressing out excess liquid.

Meanwhile, melt butter in large ovenproof skillet*. Add onion; cook over medium-low heat until
soft, about 5 minutes. Beat eggs, cheese and seasonings together. Stir in drained lettuce. Pour mixture
over onion in skillet. Cook over medium-low heat
until eggs are set, 8 to 10 minutes.

Bake at 350° 10 to 12 minutes or until knife inserted in center comes out clean and top is lightly
browned. Cut in wedges to serve.

4 servings

* To make handle ovenproof, cover completely with foil.

EGGS PROVENCALE

24 thin slices white bread, crusts removed
⅓ cup butter
1 medium tomato
¼ cup diced green pepper
¼ cup finely chopped green onion
6 eggs
Salt and pepper to taste
½ cup diced cooked ham or flaked smoked fish

Melt butter in 2-quart glass baking dish in microwave oven *1 minute at High*.

Preheat oven to 350°. Brush some of melted butter over bread. Press slices in muffin cups (2¼ to 2½ inches). Bake 10 to 15 minutes or until crisp and brown.

Meanwhile, pierce tomato skin in several places. Wrap loosely in heavy-duty plastic wrap. Cook in microwave oven *2 minutes at High*. Let stand 1 minute. Add green pepper and green onion to butter remaining in dish. Cook *1 minute at High*. Peel, core and chop tomato; add to dish with pepper and onion. Cook *1 minute at High*. Combine eggs and salt and pepper to taste; beat slightly. Add to cooked vegetables; mix well. Cook *2½ to 3 minutes at High*; stir every minute. Add ham for last 30 to 60 seconds. Spoon about 2 tablespoons mixture into each toast cup.

24 filled toast cups

MEATS AND POULTRY

TURKEY POT PIE

3 tablespoons butter
2 cups 1-inch carrot pieces (halve very large pieces)
2 cups 1-inch fresh green bean pieces
1 cup diced onion
1 clove garlic, minced
1 cup sliced fresh mushrooms
3 tablespoons cornstarch
2 cups turkey or chicken broth
1/4 teaspoon dried thyme leaves, crushed
1/4 teaspoon dried oregano leaves, crushed
1/2 teaspoon salt
1/8 teaspoon pepper
2 cups cooked turkey strips
Pastry for 1-crust pie

Preheat oven to 375°. Put butter, carrots, green beans, onion and garlic into 2-quart glass casserole. Cover. Cook in microwave oven *6 to 8 minutes at High* or until crisp-tender. Add mushrooms. Cook covered *2 minutes at High*. Set vegetables aside.

Combine cornstarch and broth in same casserole. Stir in thyme, oregano, salt and pepper. Cook in microwave oven *4 to 5 minutes at High* or until thickened; stir twice. Remove from oven. Stir in turkey and vegetable mixture. Turn into 1½-quart baking dish.

Roll out pastry to fit on top of turkey mixture. Cut slits in pastry to permit steam to escape during baking. Place pastry on filling. Seal and flute edges.

Bake at 375° 40 to 45 minutes or until crust is golden brown.
6 servings

LAMB QUICHE

Pastry shell for 9-inch quiche dish or deep 9-inch
  pie plate
1½ cups ground cooked lamb
½ cup finely chopped onion
1 tablespoon butter
1½ cups shredded Swiss cheese
1 tablespoon flour
4 eggs
1 cup half-and-half
1 teaspoon salt
Few drops liquid hot pepper sauce
¼ teaspoon dry mustard
⅛ teaspoon ground nutmeg

Preheat oven to 450°. Bake pastry 5 to 10 minutes or
until done. Remove pastry shell from oven. Sprinkle lamb evenly over bottom of shell. Set aside.

    Place onion and butter in 2-cup glass measuring
cup. Cook in microwave oven *2 minutes at High*;
stir once. Sprinkle onion evenly over lamb. Combine cheese and flour; sprinkle over onion. Combine eggs, half-and-half, salt, hot pepper sauce,
mustard and nutmeg; beat thoroughly. Pour egg
mixture over all in pastry shell.

    Cook in microwave oven *8 to 10 minutes at High*
or until knife inserted in center comes out clean;
rotate ½ turn after 4 minutes. Cut into wedges.
Serve immediately.

6 servings

CHICKEN FLORENTINE

1 package (10 ounces) frozen chopped spinach
½ teaspoon onion powder
3 cups cooked rice
2 tablespoons butter or margarine
3 tablespoons flour
1 teaspoon salt
¼ teaspoon seasoned pepper
1½ cups milk
½ cup half-and-half
2 cups coarsely chopped cooked chicken
½ cup grated Parmesan cheese
Paprika

Preheat oven to 350°. Cook spinach as directed on package, adding onion powder; drain well. Mix spinach with rice. Turn mixture into buttered 2-quart baking dish. Melt butter in saucepan. Blend in flour, salt and seasoned pepper. Add milk and half-and-half gradually, stirring constantly. Bring to boil. Cook and stir until smooth and thickened. Add chicken and half of cheese. Heat until cheese is melted. Spoon over spinach mixture in dish. Sprinkle with remaining cheese and paprika.

Bake at 350° 15 to 18 minutes or until hot and bubbly.

6 servings

PORK LOIN ROAST
(photo on cover)

1 pork loin roast (about 6 pounds)
Spiced Crab Apple Sauce (see following page)

Preheat oven to 325°. Place roast fat-side-up on rack in shallow roasting pan. Insert roast meat thermometer, so that tip is centered in thickest part. Be sure that tip does not rest in fat or on bone.

Roast in 325° oven until thermometer registers 170°. Allow 30 to 35 minutes per pound for center loin roast; 35 to 40 minutes per pound for half loin; 40 to 45 minutes per pound for blade or sirloin roast.

6 to 8 servings

Note: Have meat retailer loosen chine (back) bone by sawing across rib bones. When roasting is done, back bone can be removed easily by running carving knife along edge of roast before meat is placed on platter to be carved.

SPICED CRAB APPLE SAUCE

2 tablespoons cornstarch
1 teaspoon sugar
½ teaspoon ground cardamom
½ teaspoon salt
1 jar (16 ounces) spiced crab apples
1 cup orange juice
1 tablespoon lemon juice
1 teaspoon coarsely shredded orange peel
¼ cup golden raisins, plumped

Combine cornstarch, sugar, cardamom and salt in saucepan. Drain crab apples. Stir syrup into cornstarch mixture. Reserve crab apples to garnish pork roast platter. Add orange juice, lemon juice and orange peel to saucepan. Cook and stir over medium heat until thickened. Reduce heat. Cook slowly 2 to 3 minutes. Remove from heat. Stir in raisins. Serve with roast pork.

2 cups sauce

ONION SAUSAGE SNACKS

½ pound bulk pork sausage
1 medium sweet Spanish onion, finely chopped
1 cup commercially prepared buttermilk baking
  mix
½ teaspoon salt
4 eggs, beaten
⅓ cup vegetable oil
1 cup finely shredded Cheddar cheese
2 tablespoons minced parsley

Brown pork sausage in large skillet on medium-high heat, breaking apart to crumble with wooden spoon, about 7 minutes. Drain. Add onion, baking mix, salt, eggs, oil, cheese and parsley. Mix well. Spread mixture in greased 13x9x2-inch baking pan.

Bake at 350° 30 to 35 minutes or until golden brown. Let stand 5 minutes before cutting into squares.

About 4 dozen appetizers

FISH AND SEAFOOD

CREAMED SCALLOP-TOPPED MUFFINS

2 tablespoons butter
12 ounces fresh or thawed frozen scallops, drained
¼ cup all-purpose flour
1½ cups milk
1 can (4 ounces) sliced mushrooms (undrained)
¼ cup chopped green onion
1 teaspoon grated lemon peel
⅛ teaspoon ground nutmeg
⅛ teaspoon garlic powder
3 English muffins, halved and toasted
6 tomato slices
½ cup shredded Cheddar cheese

Preheat oven to 350°. Melt butter in 9-inch skillet. Add scallops. Saute on medium-high heat about 4 minutes, or until scallops are tender. Remove scallops with slotted spoon and set aside. Stir flour into juices in skillet. Add milk gradually, stirring constantly. Cook and stir until smooth. Add mushrooms with liquid, onion, lemon peel, nutmeg and garlic powder. Bring to boil and cook 1 minute. Stir in cooked scallops. Keep warm.

Top each toasted English muffin half with 1 tomato slice. Top evenly with cheese. Arrange on cookie sheet.

Bake at 350° 5 to 10 minutes or just until cheese is melted. Transfer muffins to serving plate and top with creamed scallops.

6 servings

SALMON LOAF WITH CUCUMBER SAUCE
(photo in color section)

2 cans (15½ ounces each) red salmon
3 eggs, beaten
⅓ cup milk
3 cups fresh bread crumbs
2 tablespoons grated onion
½ teaspoon salt
2 cups chopped pared and seeded cucumber
⅔ cup finely shredded carrot
Cucumber Sauce (see following page)

Preheat oven to 350°. Drain and flake salmon. Set aside. Beat eggs in bowl. Add milk, bread crumbs, onion and salt. Mix well. Stir in salmon, cucumber and carrot. Turn mixture into well-greased 8½x 4½x2-inch loaf pan.

Bake at 350° 1 hour 15 minutes or until center is firm. Cool 10 minutes in pan. Loosen edges with knife and turn out onto serving platter. Serve with sauce.

8 servings

CUCUMBER SAUCE

2 tablespoons butter or margarine
2 tablespoons flour
½ teaspoon salt
1½ cups milk
⅓ cup grated pared and seeded cucumber
2 tablespoons lemon juice

Melt butter in medium saucepan. Blend in flour and salt. Add milk gradually, stirring constantly. Bring to boiling. Cook and stir until sauce is thickened. Stir in cucumber and lemon juice.

About 2 cups sauce

ONE-DISH MEALS AND CASSEROLES

BRUNCH-TIME BACON BAKE

1 pound sliced bacon
1 medium onion, finely chopped
3 cups cooked rice
¼ cup all-purpose flour
2½ cups milk
½ cup grated Parmesan cheese
⅛ teaspoon pepper
2 small zucchini, coarsely shredded
⅓ cup sliced ripe olives

Cut bacon crosswise into 1-inch pieces. Cook in large skillet over medium heat until crisp. Remove bacon to absorbent paper. Reserve 3 tablespoons drippings. Return 1 tablespoon drippings to skillet. Add onion and cook until transparent.

Spread rice in 2-quart baking dish. Top with half of bacon and onion. Combine flour and remaining 2 tablespoons drippings in 1½-quart saucepan; mix well. Add milk gradually and cook over medium heat until sauce is thickened and bubbly, stirring constantly. Stir in cheese and pepper. Pour 1 cup of sauce over bacon and rice in dish. Top with zucchini and olives. Sprinkle with remaining bacon and onion; pour remaining sauce over top. Cover tightly with aluminum foil. Refrigerate overnight.

Preheat oven to 375°. Remove baking dish from refrigerator. Let stand at room temperature 15 minutes.

Bake at 375° 25 minutes. Remove foil and continue to bake 20 minutes.

6 to 8 servings

BACON-CORNBREAD DRESSING
(photo on cover)

1 pan Cornbread (see Breads), cooled and crumbled
6 cups dry ½-inch bread cubes (about 14 slices)
1 can (16 ounces) whole kernel golden corn, drained
1 chicken bouillon cube
1½ cups boiling water
12 slices bacon, cut in ¾-inch pieces
2 cups sliced celery
1 bunch green onions including 3 inches green tops, sliced
1 medium onion, finely diced
1 tablespoon poultry seasoning
½ teaspoon salt
¼ teaspoon pepper
3 eggs, beaten
½ cup butter or margarine, melted

Preheat oven to 325°. Mix crumbled cornbread, bread cubes and corn in very large bowl. Dissolve bouillon cube in boiling water. Set aside.

Put bacon into 2-quart glass measuring pitcher. Cook in microwave oven *10 to 12 minutes at High* or until crisp; stir once. Remove bacon with slotted spoon. Drain on absorbent paper. Add celery, green onions, onion, poultry seasoning, salt and pepper to bacon drippings in pitcher. Cook *5 to 6 minutes at High* or until tender. Add vegetables and bouillon to bread mixture in bowl; toss lightly. Add eggs, melted butter and cooked bacon; toss lightly until mixed. Turn dressing into 3-quart casserole. Cover tightly.

Bake at 325° 40 minutes. Remove cover. Continue baking 20 minutes.

2½ quarts dressing

SPANISH TREASURE CASSEROLE

1 cup all-purpose flour
2 teaspoons baking powder
¼ teaspoon salt
3 tablespoons shortening
8 ounces Cheddar cheese, shredded, divided
1½ cups milk, divided
6 cups sliced sweet Spanish onions
2 tablespoons butter
1 cup diced ham
1 egg
1 teaspoon prepared mustard
Parsley for garnish

Preheat oven to 450°. Combine flour, baking powder and salt in bowl. Cut in shortening and ½ cup shredded cheese with pastry blender or 2 knives until pieces are size of small peas. Add ½ cup milk all at once. Stir just until moistened. Spread in greased 2-quart baking dish.

Put onions and butter into 2-quart glass measuring pitcher. Cook in microwave oven *4 to 5 minutes at High* or until onions are limp. Stir in ham. Turn mixture into baking dish. Top with remaining cheese. Beat remaining 1 cup milk, egg and mustard. Pour over onion mixture.

Bake at 450° 10 minutes. Reduce heat to 350° and bake 20 minutes. Garnish with parsley.

6 to 8 servings

BUDGET NOODLE CASSEROLE

1 pound ground beef
1/3 cup sliced green onion
1/3 cup chopped green pepper
1/2 teaspoon salt, divided
1 can (6 ounces) tomato paste
1/2 cup dairy sour cream
1/4 teaspoon sugar
1 package (8 ounces) medium noodles, cooked and
    drained
1 cup cottage cheese
1 can (8 ounces) tomato sauce

Preheat oven to 325°. Combine ground beef, green onion and green pepper in 2-quart glass measuring pitcher. Cover with waxed paper. Cook in microwave oven *4 minutes at High* or until meat is no longer pink; stir and break meat apart with wooden spoon once. Drain off fat. Stir in 1/4 teaspoon salt.

Combine tomato paste, sour cream, sugar and remaining 1/4 teaspoon salt in large bowl; add noodles and cottage cheese. Toss well. Layer half of noodle mixture in 2-quart casserole, then half of meat mixture. Add remaining noodle mixture and top with remaining meat mixture. Pour tomato sauce over all.

Bake at 325° 30 to 35 minutes or until thoroughly heated.

6 to 8 servings

DESSERTS

PRALINE PEACH PIE

3 packages (16 ounces each) frozen unsweetened
   peach slices
2 teaspoons lemon juice
¾ cup packed light brown sugar
3 tablespoons flour
⅛ teaspoon salt
½ cup chopped pecans
Pastry for 2-crust 9-inch pie

Thaw frozen peaches in 1-quart glass measuring
pitcher in microwave oven 4 to 6 minutes at High.
Let stand 5 minutes. Drain. Put drained peaches in
large bowl. Add lemon juice, brown sugar, flour, salt
and pecans. Mix gently. Set aside.

   Preheat oven to 425°. Roll out ½ of pastry. Line 9-
inch pie plate. Trim overhang to 1 inch. Turn filling
into lined pie plate. Roll out remaining ½ of pastry.
Place on fruit. Seal and flute edge. Make 3 or 4 small
slits in top crust.

   Bake at 425° 40 to 45 minutes or until pastry is
browned. If pastry edge becomes too brown, shield
with foil. Serve warm or cool.

6 to 8 servings

APPLE-WALNUT CAKE
(photo on cover)

1⅓ cups packed brown sugar
½ cup butter or margarine
1 teaspoon vanilla extract
3 eggs
2¼ cups all-purpose flour
½ cup enriched yellow cornmeal
1 tablespoon baking powder
2 teaspoons ground cinnamon
1 teaspoon salt
½ teaspoon ground nutmeg
⅔ cup dairy sour cream
1¼ cups packed shredded pared apple
¾ cup finely chopped walnuts
Browned Butter Frosting (see recipe)
Chopped walnuts for top, if desired

Preheat oven to 350°. Beat brown sugar, butter and vanilla extract in large mixer bowl at medium speed of electric mixer 3 minutes or until light and fluffy. Add eggs, one at a time, beating well after each addition. Combine flour, cornmeal, baking powder, cinnamon, salt and nutmeg. Add alternately with sour cream to creamed mixture, mixing well after each addition. Fold in apple and ¾ cup finely chopped walnuts. Spoon batter into well-greased 9-cup Bundt pan.

Bake at 350° about 1 hour or until wooden pick inserted in center comes out clean. Cool 10 minutes. Remove cake from pan. Cool on rack. Spread Browned Butter Frosting over top of cooled cake. If desired, top with chopped walnuts.

12 servings

BROWNED BUTTER FROSTING

2 tablespoons butter
1 cup confectioners' sugar
4 to 6 teaspoons milk

Cook butter in 1-quart glass measuring pitcher in microwave oven *30 to 60 seconds at High* or until lightly browned. Remove from oven. Using whisk, mix in confectioners' sugar and enough milk for desired consistency of frosting.

[7]

Whole Meal Complementary Cooking

While complementary cooking lends itself to many single-item dishes, it also is useful in whole meal planning. First, simply having the cooking options of a microwave oven and conventional range almost automatically make meal planning easier and more interesting. With only a conventional range, many's the cook who, in the midst of preparing a meal, runs out of surface units or oven space, or can't use the broiler because the oven's in use. Or the cook who was detained on the way home and now doesn't have time to cook the roast that was planned for dinner; or who discovers halfway through meal preparation that a key ingredient is still in the freezer. The flexibility of a choice of cooking appliances makes problems such as these a thing of the past.

The chart on pages 103 to 115 is a useful tool in menu planning and timing. A look can quickly help determine which portions of the meal should be cooked in which appliance. It also can help to set up a rough timetable. A meatloaf, for example, can be cooked equally well in a conventional, convection or microwave oven. If you have the time, you may prefer to prepare the meatloaf and let it cook in the regular oven. If time is short, the microwave oven would be the best choice.

A holiday menu, including appropriate recipes, based on Whole Meal Complementary Cooking follows. The meal is timed, for several reasons: Timing is the part of meal preparation that many cooks find most difficult, particularly when becoming familiar with new types of appliances. And the times illustrate the substantial savings in meal preparation time by utilizing each type of appliance to its best advantage. This menu and recipes should be a springboard to more efficient cooking and tasty, nutritious meals made possible by the concept of complementary cooking.

MENU

Roast Turkey
Corn Bread, Mushroom and Sausage Stuffing
Candied Sweet Potatoes with Mandarin Oranges
Traditional Vegetable Platter with Cheese Sauce
Cranberry Sauce   Relishes
Rolls and Butter
Apple Mince Pie with Rum Butter Sauce
Coffee
(Serves 8)

MARKET ORDER

1 (13-pound) turkey
1 pound pork sausage
6 large Roman Beauty, Winesap or Red Delicious
    apples
1 cauliflower (about 1 pound 3 ounces)
1 orange
1 (1-pound) package fresh cranberries
Celery
6 sweet potatoes
1 medium onion
1 pound fresh mushrooms
Assorted relishes for relish tray
16-24 ounces prepared mincemeat
1 package pastry mix
2 (8½-ounce) packages corn bread mix
1 (8-ounce) can mandarin oranges
1 quart dry bread cubes
1 (10-ounce) package frozen green beans
1 (10-ounce) package frozen peas and carrots
1 (10-ounce) package frozen corn
¾ cup shredded process or natural Cheddar cheese
Rolls
1½ sticks butter
3 eggs
Milk
1¾ cups sugar
2 tablespoons flour
½ cup brown sugar
⅓ cup slivered almonds
Ground ginger
Onion powder
Sage

Dry mustard
Paprika
Salt
Pepper
⅓ cup rum

Day before the Feast:

1:00 p.m. Prepare and cook apples for pie (microwave). Pare six large or 10 small apples into sixths (if using small apples, cut into quarters); place in a single layer in a 10-inch glass pie plate. Cut 2 tablespoons butter into small chunks and scatter over apples; sprinkle ¼ cup sugar and 1 teaspoon shredded orange peel over apples. Cover with plastic wrap and microwave at full power for 1½ to 3 minutes or until apples are tender but not mushy. Turn plate once. Cook, stirring occasionally.

1:30 p.m. Defrost turkey: Begin defrosting turkey in microwave oven following manufacturer's directions.

1:45 p.m. Prepare pie crust: Prepare pie crust to fit two (9-inch) pie plates. Use a package mix or favorite pastry recipe. Line pie plates with pastry. Refrigerate.

2:00 p.m. Turn turkey as directed.

2:10 p.m. Prepare corn bread: Prepare two packages corn bread mix according to package directions. Put in a 13x9-inch pan. (Favorite corn bread recipe may be used.)

2:30 p.m. Turn turkey as directed.

2:45 p.m. Bake corn bread according to package directions. Bake six sweet potatoes in oven with corn bread until tender, about 40-45 minutes.

2:50 p.m. Finish preparation of pie: Remove

pie shells from refrigerator. Drain apples and
arrange in pie shells, using half in each. Spoon 2-3
cups mincemeat in pie shells, using half in each and.
spread.

3:00 p.m.   Turn turkey as directed.

3:25 p.m.   Remove corn bread and sweet potatoes from oven.

3:30 p.m.   Turn turkey as directed.

3:40 p.m.   Bake pie: Bake pie in a 450° F oven
for 10 minutes; reduce heat to 350° F and bake for 15
minutes or until brown and bubbly.

3:45 p.m.   Cook cranberries: Wash and pick
through cranberries. Put 1 cup water or orange juice
and 1 cup sugar in a 3-quart saucepan. Place on surface unit and bring to a boil; add cranberries and 1
tablespoon grated orange rind. Bring to a boil and
cook until skins pop; cool. Cover and refrigerate.

4:00 p.m.   Turkey should be defrosted: Wash
under cold water.

4:05 p.m.   Remove pie from oven—cool: Remove giblets from turkey. Refrigerate turkey until
time to stuff.

4:15 p.m.   Cook giblets in 1 quart of water and
¼ teaspoon salt until tender. Giblets may be used
in gravy. Broth is used in gravy and stuffing.

4:20 p.m.   Start stuffing: Microwave pork
sausage at full power in a 10-inch glass pie plate
covered with a paper towel for six to eight minutes,
stirring once or twice. Crumble cooled corn bread
(about 12 cups) in a large bowl. Add 1 quart dry
bread cubes. Remove cooked sausage with a slotted
spoon and add to bread. Leave 2 tablespoons fat in
pie pan. Add fresh mushrooms (sliced), ½ cup
chopped onion and ½ cup chopped celery to drip-

pings. Cover pie plate with plastic wrap and micro-wave at full power for three minutes, stirring once or twice. Add mushroom mixture to sausage and bread; mix.

4:35 p.m. Start preparing favorite relishes: Wrap in plastic wrap and refrigerate.

5:00 p.m. Store pie. Finish stuffing: Add two beaten eggs and enough turkey broth (about 2 cups) to moisten stuffing as desired. Refrigerate. (Will stuff a 12-13 pound turkey.)

Day of the Feast:

9:30 a.m. Remove turkey and dressing from refrigerator.

Prepare sweet potato casserole and make syrup for potatoes: Peel six baked sweet potatoes and slice into thick slices. Drain mandarin oranges, reserve juice. Layer potatoes, mandarin oranges and ⅓ cup slivered almonds in a 2-quart low casserole. Put ½ cup packed brown sugar, 4 tablespoons butter, ¼ teaspoon salt, ¼ teaspoon ground ginger and ¼ cup juice into 2-cup glass pitcher. Microwave at full power for about 1½ minutes or until hot and melt-ed. Pour syrup over potatoes.

10:00 a.m. Stuff and truss turkey: Extra stuff-ing may be baked alongside turkey.

11:00 a.m. Put turkey in conventional or con-vection oven. Follow manufacturer's directions for baking a 13-pound turkey.

11:15 a.m. Set table and prepare serving dishes. Enjoy some of the day knowing everything is under control!

2:00 p.m. Make rum butter sauce for pie: Put ⅓ cup butter into a 2-cup measuring pitcher. Melt in microwave oven on full power, about 1 minute. Stir ½ cup sugar into 1 beaten egg; whisk into hot butter. Microwave on full power for 1½ minutes, beating once or twice with a whisk. Cool slightly and stir in ⅓ cup rum.

2:45 p.m. Put sweet potatoes in oven with turkey: (Bake for about 25 minutes).

3:00 p.m. Begin cooking cauliflower: Place 1 cauliflower (about 1-pound, 3-ounces) cored and trimmed, stem down in a 2-quart glass casserole. Add ¼ cup water and cover. Microwave on full power for six minutes, turning once or place on turntable. Remove from microwave oven. Prepare vegetables: Arrange ½ (10-ounce) package frozen green beans, ½ (10-ounce) package peas and carrots and ½ (10-ounce) package frozen corn in three sections on a 12-inch platter that is microwave safe. Cover with plastic wrap.

3:10 p.m. Remove turkey from oven: Put pie in oven with sweet potatoes and turn off heat.

3:15 p.m. Microwave vegetables at full power for eight minutes, turning the platter twice. Remove from microwave oven. Place cauliflower in center of platter; cover with plastic wrap.

3:30 p.m. Make cheese sauce for vegetables: Place 2 tablespoons butter in a 4-cup glass pitcher; microwave at full power for 45 seconds or until butter melts. Blend in 2 tablespoons flour, ⅛ teaspoon onion powder; ⅛ teaspoon pepper and ¼ teaspoon dry mustard. Microwave on full power for 30 seconds. Whisk in 1 cup milk until well blended; microwave on full power for three minutes until mixture thickens and bubbles. Remove from microwave oven and whisk to blend; add ¾ cup shredded process or natural Cheddar cheese and microwave on full power for 30 seconds. Remove from microwave and whisk till smooth.

3:40 p.m. Put turkey on platter.

3:45 p.m. Make gravy with drippings in turkey pan.

3:55 p.m. Return covered vegetables to microwave oven and microwave at full power for two minutes. Remove plastic from vegetables and pour sauce over them. Sprinkle with paprika and serve.

3:58 p.m. Warm rolls in microwave oven for 30-60 seconds.

4:00 p.m. Serve dinner.

Dessert time: Make coffee; heat sauce in microwave oven for pie.

[8]

Kitchen Design and Arrangement

Few vestiges of the 1930s and 1940s can function to today's standards of performance. For instance, a 1932 Chevrolet might be a great collector's item, but hardly the car for dependable transportation on today's fast-moving freeways. And, automatic dishwashers and microwave ovens hadn't even been invented.

What does this mean for the kitchen? It means that a kitchen planned for the typical family of 50, 30 or even 10 years ago just won't work as well for today's living patterns.

Kitchen concepts need to fit the lifestyles of married couples who like to prepare dinner together; or the one-person household that doesn't need a huge kitchen. And certainly, the frazzled working man or woman who comes home from work and prepares a meal for children in a half hour or 45 minutes has to have a kitchen that can help do the cooking chores as fast and efficiently as possible.

Space is a big factor in today's kitchen planning, too. With the trend toward smaller homes and smaller kitchens, space has to be better planned to include all the necessary "tools" to make the kitchen work efficiently. In some outdated kitchens that may mean simply reorganizing what's stored. In other kitchens, where extensive remodeling or adding new appliances isn't possible, sometimes a modest remodeling project can result in big improvements in efficiency without a serious strain on finances.

There are many ways to alter kitchen design and make it keep pace with today's lifestyle. Here's the latest thinking on kitchen planning, incorporating changes in available materials and appliances, plus changes in lifestyles and cooking patterns.

TWO COOKS IN THE KITCHEN

Too many cooks spoil the broth? Not anymore. More than one person cooking is time-saving, work-saving and a nice way to be together.

If a kitchen is short on space, one way to accommodate a second cook might be a complete cooking center with a full-size conventional range and microwave oven all in a 30-inch space. Counter space on each side of the range lets two cooks work at the same time.

Another successful strategy in a kitchen that includes a microwave oven is to separate the microwave oven from the conventional range by at least four feet. With the microwave oven near the refrigerator, one cook can prepare a salad and vegetables while the other is at the range cooking.

Traffic congestion can be relieved in a two-cook kitchen by equipping work centers with duplicate tools. Plan for two sets of measuring cups, knives and cooking utensils.

If remodeling is a possibility, plan a wider aisle

in a corridor kitchen or maximum dimensions between the range, refrigerator and clean-up center.

A KITCHEN EATING AREA

Snacks, quick meals, staggered eating times, informal living—they're all geared to an eat-in kitchen.

If a space-wasting, old-fashioned table-and-chairs dining arrangement won't fit, look at some of these alternatives:

A Counter   Add a counter perpendicular to the wall of an "L"-shaped kitchen or wrap a counter around a kitchen island.

Attached Table   A rectangular table can be attached to a dividing counter or a kitchen island.

Custom-made Table   If there's an unused corner, alcove or sliver of wall, design a banquette or booth to fill the space.

When planning an eating area, allow 21 to 24 inches for each place setting.

AN OPEN-SPACE KITCHEN

Why isolate cooking from other family activities? An open kitchen combines food preparation, eating, TV, reading or just enjoying family members being together.

Before removing walls, consider these things:

Noise Control   Minimize noise from the kitchen by selecting appliances that operate quietly. Nothing disturbs the ambiance of a kitchen/family room like a noisy dishwasher or food waste disposer. Look for models that feature quiet operation.

Lighting   Equip the kitchen with good, strong lighting for work centers. The other areas of the open room need softer, more intimate lighting. With multiple switching on light fixtures, rheostats and dimmers on incandescent lamps and alternating switching on fluorescent lamps, you can create almost any lighting effect.

Odor Control   Plan kitchen ventilation carefully. Properly installed ventilating equipment effectively removes odors plus smoke and excess heat and moisture.

WHICH SHAPE TO CHOOSE

There's an alphabet soup choice of kitchen shapes, but it all boils down to creating a workable triangle between range, refrigerator and sink/dishwasher. Shorten the legs of the work triangle to save steps. Lengthen them to make room for more than one cook at a time.

There are a variety of kitchen layouts, each with its own advantage, depending on the desired function of the kitchen. Think about family size, who cooks, what kind of cooking and entertaining are done and where household members eat.

A Corridor Kitchen   offers one cook the advantage of an efficient, close grouping of work centers on parallel walls. However, household traffic may cross back and forth through the area and usually it is cramped for two cooks unless you can stretch the width of the aisle between the two working walls.

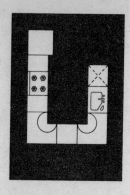

"U"-shaped

"U"-shaped Kitchen   surrounds the cook on three sides with continuous countertop and directs walk-through traffic out of the work area. This arrangement is a good choice for one person who wants to handle kitchen chores in the most efficient way possible.

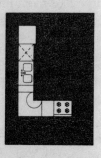

"L"-shaped

"L"-shaped Kitchen   gives the cook a generous amount of continuous counter space though generally less than a "U"-shaped area. With work centers on two adjacent walls a natural triangle is formed and traffic bypasses the area. This layout is the most accommodating for two or more cooks and often allows space for an island or dining area.

One-wall Kitchen   has all work centers stretched along a single wall. This is the least efficient kitchen design and its only benefit is it gives its occupant plenty of exercise.

"G"-shaped Kitchen   is a new approach gaining popularity. It is an extension of the U-shape, with an extra wall for cabinets and appliances. What happens here is the tighter work triangle of the U-shaped kitchen is loosened up and expanded, making the area comfortable for more people or activities.

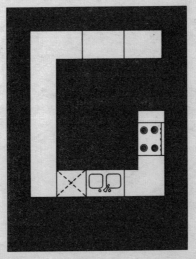

"G"-shaped

AN ISLAND OF EFFICIENCY

As a counter space-stretcher, an island is tops. It also can improve the function of the kitchen by housing the range or sink and dishwasher.

Before planning an island, take a look at the kitchen's work triangle. There should be not less than four feet between any two work centers—refrigerator, sink and range. If, by adding an island, traffic is obstructed between any points of the triangle, the addition would be more of a headache than a help. Consider adding counter work space with pull-out cutting boards in cabinets or a roll-around work cart parked in an adjacent room during off-duty hours.

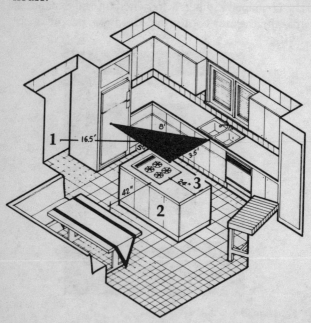

1.   Total measurements of a good work triangle should be no less than 12 feet and no more than 21 feet. A kitchen that is too large is just as inconvenient as a kitchen that is too small.

2.   Allow clearance around an island. A minimum of 36 to 42 inch clearance is needed from the edge of the island to opposite cabinets, appliances, walls or tables. Make certain there's enough clearance to open appliance and cabinet doors.

3.   To install a cooktop in an island, allow a minimum space of 12 to 18 inches for countertops on either side of the cooking unit. To equip an island as a clean-up center, 24 inches in width is needed for a dishwasher and 33 to 36 inches for a double sink, plus additional work surface as needed.

[9]

Kitchen Appliances

The appliances you choose, where they are placed and how they are used can be the winning combination in a time-saving, work-saving kitchen. Some appliances save time and work; others are designed to save space.

CHOOSING THE BEST PLACE FOR YOUR MICROWAVE OVEN

Most kitchens of even a few years ago didn't have microwave ovens, so naturally no special space was planned for them. Finding a spot for the microwave oven in a kitchen is a challenge for two reasons: Space often is at a premium; and there is no one "best" spot—it depends on the kitchen-use patterns of each household.

Initially, microwave ovens were referred to as "portable." They were simply placed on a countertop, much like a toaster oven (but much bigger). This installation is undesirable for several reasons:

154

- The oven placement often is determined by available counter space, rather than by usage considerations.
- Counter space—usually at a premium also—is sacrificed.
- The countertop surface under the microwave oven can't be cleaned without moving the 70 to 100 pound unit.
- The size of the oven is visually unattractive.

Many other locations and installations now are being used by kitchen planners. When selecting the proper location for a microwave oven, first consider these points:

- If the unit will be used by the principal cook during normal food preparation activities, it must be placed within the work triangle.
- If the unit will be used mainly by other family members, or by a second cook, it can—and usually should—be located away from the primary cook's work triangle.

With those points in mind, consider these locations:

The Food Preparation and Mixing Center— usually between the refrigerator and sink. Many of the uses for a microwave oven take place in this area —defrosting, preparing and cooking fresh vegetables, preparing snacks, reconstituting foods, and other general food preparation and cooking. This is an ideal location if two family members often share the cooking. One cook can be working in the food preparation area; the second in the cooking area.

Microwave oven placement

The Cooking Center   When the main function of the oven will be to augment surface unit and oven cooking, this is often the best location, particularly if there is just one primary cook. But keep in mind: the microwave oven far more frequently replaces surface unit cooking than it does oven cooking. It also is a use-intensive appliance much like a cooktop. With a conventional oven, foods often go in and cook for an hour or more with no more than an occasional "peek." A microwave oven, much like surface units, requires more attention during most cooking processes. Therefore, the microwave oven should be placed close to the cooktop, and not in the remote location that often works well for a separate conventional oven.

The Serving Area   When the microwave oven will be used primarily for heating or reheating—as many are—this often is the most convenient location. It is out of the "mainstream" kitchen, and space may be less at a premium.

Now, consider the second important point:

WHAT HEIGHT?

Research has pointed up two considerations: For convenience, the oven's cooking shelf should be from two inches below to ten inches above elbow height. For safety, the shelf should be no higher than the user's shoulder.

How does this translate into normal kitchen installations? It means that microwave ovens installed at countertop height, or as part of a built-in oven bank, usually fall within this height range. Units built in to be flush with the bottom of adjacent wall cabinets are a bit high for the average female user. (For a person 5′ 5″ tall, the average elbow height is 39 inches; shoulder height, 52 inches—wall cabinets usually start at about 54 inches from the floor.)

If finding space for the microwave oven is a problem, consider these locations that may not have been thought of:

• Recess the microwave oven into the wall behind it. This could be the wall behind the food preparation area; near a built-in oven; or a side wall of your kitchen. Ventilation, structural and electrical requirements must be considered, of course, before simply "sinking" a microwave oven into a wall.

• Install the microwave oven in a custom wall cabinet at convenient use height. Often, this can be coupled with a conventional wall oven, a space-saving design if it places the microwave oven in a convenient location in the kitchen.

• Installing a microwave oven at countertop height or wall cabinet base height is practical, but raises aesthetic considerations: Because the microwave oven usually is deeper than the cabinets above, it intrudes into the kitchen visually. Here are two ways to correct that problem:

• Recess the oven just a few inches into the wall behind.

• Place the microwave oven next to the refrigerator so there's no visual jarring note. This location is good in terms of what a microwave oven often is used for. And, unlike a conventional oven, the "cool cooking" of a microwave oven doesn't dictate that it be separated from the refrigerator for the sake of energy conservation.

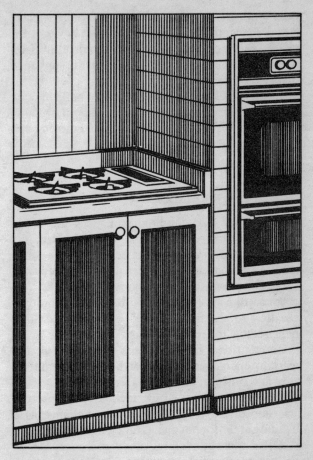

Built-in appliances

BENEFITS OF BUILT-INS

One successful way to increase cabinet storage in remodeling or appliance replacement is to consider built-ins. A built-in cooktop drops neatly into a countertop, leaving the cabinet below it for storage that a conventional range would eliminate. A built-in cooktop is a trim, space-saving appliance that also can be installed in an island.

Combine a built-in cooktop with a built-in oven for a team of cabinet conservationists. If space is limited within work centers, install a built-in oven outside the work triangle.

BUILT-IN OVEN LOCATION

Conventional free-standing appliances are comfortable for average-size persons to work with, but not for very tall or very short cooks. On the other hand, a built-in appliance can be positioned at a height convenient to an individual cook's size.

For comfort and safety, a built-in oven should be installed so the fully opened oven door is three inches below the cook's crooked elbow.

Conventional built-in ovens should not be beneath kitchen countertops. High cooking temperatures and venting can create safety hazards.

Plan a minimum of 18 inches of countertop space on at least one side of the appliance as a "landing area" for hot dishes taken from the oven.

All of these guidelines apply to convection as well as conventional (radiant heat) ovens, since both are used in similar ways.

Another appliance that gives added flexibility to kitchen planning is the down-draft grill-range or cooktop. Because no overhead exhaust hood is needed, upper cabinet storage space is gained. And the design often is aesthetically more pleasing than a range hood, particularly in a location such as an island or peninsula.

REFRIGERATOR/FREEZER

For easy loading and unloading of the refrigerator, there should be 15 to 18 inches of counter space next to the door on the side unobstructed by the open door. If it's a side-by-side model, with doors opening from the center, there should be counter space on the freezer side or on both.

DISHWASHERS

With today's fast-paced lifestyles a dishwasher is virtually a necessity. But without foresight and proper placement this convenient appliance actually can be an inconvenience in the kitchen.

It takes planning to make sure that when the dishwasher door is opened you are neither boxed-in or blocked-out. One common mistake in dishwasher installation is locating the unit adjacent to an angled corner sink, making it impossible to stand in front of the sink and load the dishwasher. Watch for this and other tight-squeeze situations. See the drawing in this chapter for installation tips to help you avoid these traps.

Here are other convenient placement tips:

• Minimize stooping and bending by elevating the dishwasher 12 to 18 inches off the floor. It makes the dishwasher easier to load and reduces the physical energy you expend. Extra storage cabinets can be added above and below the dishwasher.

• In a small kitchen that can't accommodate a

built-in dishwasher, consider a movable island to house a portable unit. The dishwasher can be stored out of the kitchen until it is needed, then rolled in at clean-up time.

1.   Clearance is important. To ensure access to the dishwasher from the sink, leave 20 inches next to the dishwasher for loading. Leave 42 inches in front of the dishwasher for door opening and closing.

2.   Proximity to dish storage saves work. If possible, arrange the kitchen so dishes and silverware are stored between the dishwasher and where they're used at mealtime. The less walking required between the dishwasher and dish storage area, the tighter, more efficient the work pattern becomes.

3.   Relationship to the sink should be considered. While most right-handed people work from left to right in the kitchen, research has shown that the dishwasher may be the exception to the rule. More often than not, a dishwasher is placed to the left of the sink.

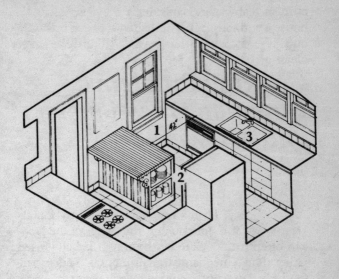

Good dishwasher placement

[10]

Cooking Problems: Common Questions— and Answers

When an appliance seems to be malfunctioning, the source of the problem often turns out to be the way it is being used rather than a mechanical malfunction. This is particularly true with cooking appliances, because there are so many variables involved: recipe selection, quality of ingredients, cooking techniques, utensil size and material, heat or power selection, to name a few.

Non-mechanical problems also tend to crop up more often when an appliance is new. Most people

Proper use of aluminum foil

assume that a new range, for example, will work just like the old one. But controls may operate differently. Heat settings or rack positions may be different. Or the problem may be that the new appliance is operating properly and the old one actually wasn't. For example, oven thermostats can drift. Over the years, as they are jarred during cooking or cleaning, or become spattered with grease, they can lose their accuracy. Most cooks adjust for this automatically, and adjust recipe timing accordingly. Then, with a new oven, with an accurate thermostat, the old recipes don't work right.

The information in this chapter covers the most common consumer questions and problems that are the result of appliance use, not mechanical malfunction. While inclusive and generic, there always will be unusual or extraordinary situations. The companion to this section should be the manual for the specific appliance. It may not have all the answers either, but should help resolve annoying problems, or help to avoid an unnecessary—and expensive—service call.

Do not block oven vent

RANGES—BAKING

Problem: Uneven Browning—Cakes, cookies and pies may not brown at all or they may brown unevenly.

Causes	Solutions
Incorrect rack position	If the rack position is too high or too low, uneven browning will occur.
Incorrect placement of pans on the rack or too many pans on one rack	Pans should not touch each other or the oven walls. Allow two inches between pans and oven walls for proper air circulation. When using both racks for baking, stagger the pans so one is not directly over another. (Too many pans on one rack will block the air flow.)
Oven not preheated or oven door opened too frequently	Fully preheat the oven to temperature called for in the recipe. Do not open the oven door before the end of the minimum recommended baking time. Opening the oven door frequently during baking allows heat to escape.
Aluminum foil used on	Aluminum foil should not be used on the rack on which the utensil is

the oven racks to keep them clean

placed as it cuts down on air circulation and radiation transfer of heat to the food. Foil may be used to catch a spillover by placing it on the rack below the utensil and rack being used for baking. Do not cover the entire rack.

Incorrect pan material. Dark or dull pans were used rather than shiny pans

Use shiny aluminum pans for cakes, cookies and biscuits when a light, delicately golden brown crust is desired. Use dull metal pans or glass when a dark or well-browned crust is desired for breads or pies. When baking cakes in a glass utensil, lower the recommended temperature by 25°F and use the recommended cooking time in the recipe. It is not necessary to lower temperatures for baking pies or cooking casseroles in glass utensils.

Incorrect pan size or too little batter in the pans

Do not use a cookie sheet so large that it touches the walls of the oven. Use the size pan recommended in the recipe. As a general guide, cake pans should be filled only about 2/3 full. Use level pans as warped ones result in uneven browning and poorly shaped products. Bake biscuits and cookies on a flat sheet or a very shallow pan. If the sheet or utensil has sides, pale or light browning will occur.

Oven vent is blocked

Check the oven vent to make sure it is not blocked, as any blockage restricts the airflow within the oven.

RANGES—BAKING *continued*

Problem: Uneven Baking—When uneven baking occurs, cakes will not rise properly, they may not be level and they may not be done in the center. Pies may have a soggy crust or the edge of the piecrust may burn.

Causes	Solutions
Range is not level	Check to see if the range is level by placing a spirit level on the oven rack itself. Make any adjustments necessary.
Oven out of calibration	Have oven thermostat calibration checked to make sure it is neither too high nor too low.
Wrong baking temperature	When the temperature is too high, cakes will not be done in the center and the edges of piecrusts may burn. If the temperature is too low, a cake may fall or the bottom crust of a pie may be soggy. Make sure the oven temperature control is set properly according to the recipe. Compare the individual recipe with other similar recipes from a standard cookbook to see if the time or temperature in the

recipe may be in error.

Pans touching each other or the oven walls	Allow at least two inches of space between pans and the oven walls for proper air.
Incorrect pan material	Use shiny aluminum pans to reflect heat and give a delicate golden brown color to cakes, cookies and biscuits. Use dark or anodized pans for pies to absorb the heat and prevent soggy crusts.
Improper pan size	A pan that is too large or too small will cause uneven baking results. Check the recipe to make sure the pan size used is the one recommended.
Warped pan	Warped or bent baking pans will cause uneven baking results and poorly shaped products.

RANGES—BROILING

Problem: Excessive Smoke—When broiling foods in the oven, excessive smoke may occasionally occur.

Causes	Solutions
A closed oven door	With an electric range broiling always is done with the door opened to the first "stop" position (opened about four inches).
Excess fat on meat	Before broiling trim excess fat to prevent excessive spattering and cut slashes around the outer edges of the meat to prevent curling during cooking.
Plugged up drainage holes in the broiler pan	Food must be placed on a broiler tray and pan to allow fat to drip to the pan below. The broiler tray always must be used with the broiler pan as fat may become hot enough to ignite if directly exposed to the heat source. If the broiler tray is lined with foil, cut openings to allow the fat to drip to the pan below.

Broiler tray and pan left in oven after broiling	Never leave a soiled broiler tray and pan in the oven after broiling. The drippings might become hot enough to ignite if exposed directly to the heat source.
Use of disposable broiler pans	Do not use disposable broiler pans as they do not provide the separate broiler tray.

Problem: Excessive Spattering & Cleanup

Causes	Solutions
Meat drippings are overheating	Always use the broiler pan and rack when broiling. A small amount of water may be added to the broiler pan.
Insufficient drainage from meat drippings	Never cover the broiler rack with foil unless holes are punched to allow for drainage.
Too much fat around the edge of the meat	Before broiling trim excess fat to prevent excessive spattering and cut slashes around the outer edges of the meat to prevent curling.

RANGES—SURFACE COOKING

Problem: Uneven Surface Cooking—When uneven surface cooking occurs, foods may burn, water may not boil as fast as it should and cooking results are generally uneven.

Causes	Solutions
Range is not level	With a spirit level check the range surface from front to back and side to side.
Pan material used	Pans should be made of a material that will evenly conduct the heat from the surface unit or burner. Medium to heavy gauge aluminum pans are excellent heat conductors. Pans with poor heat transfer capabilities may cause food to burn in spots or may require longer cooking time.
Warped pans or pans not the right size	Inspect the utensils to assure they have flat bottoms and use the proper size pan for the size of the surface unit.

Problem: Chrome Reflector Bowls Tarnish or Change Color

Causes

Excessive heat, as the result of using over-sized cookware—when canning food, for example

Failure to clean up spillovers

Solutions

This problem really cannot be avoided if oversized utensils are used and with the heat and long cooking times of canning. The reflector bowls, however, are easily replaced. To save money, take them to the dealer or service organization rather than arranging for a service call.

Various foods may cause reflector bowls to discolor if spillovers are allowed to burn on. Clean spillovers as soon as reflector bowls have cooled after cooking.

RANGES—CLEANING

Problem: Smoke During the Self-Clean Cycle—Although some slight smoking is normal, excessive smoke may be noticed coming from the range while the oven is in the self-clean operation.

Cause

Excessive grease in the oven or a utensil or foil left in the oven

Solution

Check manufacturer's recommendation for interrupting self-clean cycle. Wipe out excess spillage or remove the utensil. Start the self-cleaning oven operation again.

RANGES—CLEANING continued

Problem: Discoloration of Oven Racks—After a self-clean cycle, the racks are discolored and hard to slide on their guides in and out of the oven.

Cause

This is normal, as racks will lose their shine and become difficult to slide when exposed to the high heat of a self-cleaning cycle

Solution

Remove the oven racks prior to the self-clean cycle and wash them by hand to prevent discoloration. If they are left in the oven during the cycle, polish the edges of the racks and rack guides with soap-filled steel wool pads and rub a light layer of mineral or salad oil on edges of racks to make them easier to slide.

Problem: Continuous Clean Oven Does Not Clean

Causes

Misunderstanding about the continuous clean process

Solutions

A continuous clean oven is designed to be presentably clean—not spotless. The oven surface has a rough texture that absorbs spatters and allows them to spread, thus exposing a larger area to the hot oven air to speed the oxidation of soil.

Little roasting or baking in the oven	The continuous clean finish works best at high baking temperatures. Consumers who broil a lot and do little baking will find that the oven is not on long enough during broiling to reduce heavy build-ups of food soil. Baking at temperatures of 350°F or above is essential to achieve gradual cleaning.
Carbohydrate spills, such as pies	Continuous cleaning ovens are not designed to reduce heavy carbohydrate spills. When baking this type of food, place a cookie sheet or aluminum foil just a little larger than the pan on the rack directly below the rack holding the utensil to catch spills.
Using an oven cleaner	Chemicals from a commercial oven cleaner will clog the porous finish of a continuous clean oven, thus eliminating the cleaning action.

MICROWAVE OVENS

Problem: Uneven Cooking

Causes	Solutions
Shape of container	Use a round or ring/donut-shaped pan. Or, shield corners of a square or rectangular pan with aluminum foil.
Arrangement of food in container	Place larger, thicker portions of the food to the outside of the container and smaller, thinner portions to the center.
Placement of food in the oven	Center food if cooking a single item. Arrange several items like potatoes, cups of coffee or cupcakes in a circle around the center of the oven.
Improper handling	Use the appropriate handling techniques such as stirring, turning the dish, turning the food over, rearranging the food or the dishes. See cookbook for additional information.

Problem: Food dry and hard

Cause
Cooked too long

Solution
Use least amount of time recommended. After standing time, check doneness. Add more time if necessary. Not all foods should be cooked on Full Power. Reduce power level according to type of food. For example, beef roasts, dairy products and cheese should be cooked at lower power levels.

Problem: Food pops during cooking

Causes
Since microwave cooking is so fast, pressure quickly builds up in foods with a tight membrane, peel or skin. This will result in a "bursting" or "popping" effect.

Solutions
Cover vegetables such as peas or beans or soups to prevent splattering in the oven if food pops. Before cooking, pierce foods like potatoes, squash, tomatoes, egg yolks and chicken livers with a fork or toothpick. Also, cut a small opening in cooking bags.

High fat content

Foods like butter or chicken may pop while cooking. Use a covering to reduce spatters in the oven.

Candy/Cakes

Problem: Unevenly cooked

Causes	Solutions
Improper handling	Cakes should be rotated for even cooking results.
Improper mixing	Use a mixer to make sure all ingredients are thoroughly blended.
Wrong shaped pan	Use a round or ring/donut-shaped pan.
Pan filled too full	Fill pans with cake batter no more than ½ full.

Problem: Chocolate chips or other candy morsels will not melt

Cause	Solution
Candy morsels and bar chocolate hold their shape while heating	Stir after recommended cooking time. If not completely melted, allow standing time then microwave longer and stir again. (Note: Imitation chocolate chips usually will not provide satisfactory results.)

Eggs

Problem: Turn dark or rubbery

Causes	Solutions
Overcooked	Decrease cooking time. Remove eggs from the oven while they are still slightly undercooked. Let stand 2–3 minutes to complete cooking.
Power level too high	Eggs are considered a "critical" food and may cook better at a lower power level, about 80 percent.

Meat

Problem: Tough and dry

Causes	Solutions
Cooked too fast	Unless it is a ground beef dish, use a lower power level setting.
Cooked too long	Use minimum amount of cooking time recommended. Allow food to stand. After standing time, check for doneness. Add more time if necessary.
Salted before cooking	Do not salt meat until after cooking. Salt tends to draw moisture out of food while cooking.

Problem: When using the probe, oven shuts off before meat is done

Cause	Solution
The probe may be inserted in a fat pocket or next to a bone	Remove the probe and reinsert.

Popcorn

Problem: Does not pop

Causes	Solutions
Type of popcorn popper used	A popcorn popper with a cone-shaped base works most effectively.
Stale popcorn	Use fresh popcorn with a high moisture content. To insure freshness keep unpopped corn tightly covered and refrigerated.

[11]

Avoiding Unnecessary Service Calls

When an appliance doesn't work, it can have a disrupting impact on the entire household. When this happens, often the first reaction is to call a service firm.

There are times when a malfunctioning appliance cannot be repaired without the expertise of a trained service technician. However, it is estimated that nearly 30 percent of all service calls can be avoided if people follow a simple checklist to make certain, among other things, that controls are set properly and that the appliance is connected to adequate utility connections.

This chapter discusses ways to avoid unnecessary service calls and where to find good service when a call is necessary.

(See Chapter 10 for common questions and answers to cooking problems.)

First, here are procedures to check on appliances:

GAS AND ELECTRIC RANGES

Range Clock and/or Lights Do Not Work Is the range connected to a power supply? Is the bulb or fluorescent tube burned out? Is the switch, starter or ballast defective? If so, replace the starter or have a service technician check the switch and ballast. Have a service technician check the clock or wiring.

Gas Ranges

Surface Burner Fails to Light   Is the range connected to a power supply? Are the burner ports clogged? If so, clean them with a straight pin.

Uneven Flame   Are the burner ports clogged? If so, clean them with a straight pin. Have a service technician adjust the burner.

Surface Burner Flame Lifts Off Port, is Yellow in Color or Noisy When Turned On   Have a service technician adjust the burner. Problem is probably caused by an improper air and gas mixture.

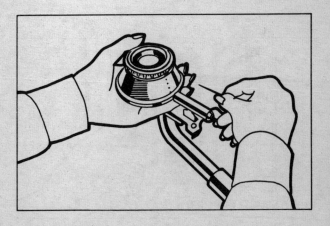

Clean gas burner ports

Oven Burner Does Not Light Is the range connected to a power supply? Will the surface burners light?

Electric Ranges

Surface or Oven Elements Fail to Turn On Is the unit plugged in? Is there a tripped circuit breaker or blown fuse? Have a service technician check the element control or for a defective element.

Oven Does Not Turn On Is the unit plugged in? Is there a tripped circuit breaker or blown fuse? Are the controls properly set? Refer to appliance manual.

Oven Door Will Not Unlock On Range Equipped With Self-clean Oven Are the controls properly set? Refer to the appliance manual. Has the oven cooled after self-clean cycle?

Check circuit breakers or fuses

Microwave Ovens

Oven Won't Operate   Is the oven plugged in? If plugged in but still doesn't work, the cause may be wiring, a fuse or circuit breaker. Is the oven door securely closed? Is the oven correctly set? Are the air vents blocked?

The oven may overheat and turn off if the air vents are blocked. Let oven cool one hour, then restart. If it still won't operate, call a service technician.

Food Takes Longer to Cook Than Suggested Times Given in Cookbook   Check the voltage. In your area, it may have fluctuated below the normal operating voltage range. Is oven operating on the same circuit with another appliance? If so, cooking times will increase when both units are on at the same time. If the oven has a removable glass tray, is it in place? If not, cooking times may be affected.

Are more or larger amounts of food being placed in the oven than called for in the recipe? If so, cooking time will increase. Is the food frozen or was it refrigerated immediately prior to placing in the oven? Some recipes reflect the times needed to cook food at room temperature.

WHEN TO CALL FOR SERVICE

If everything checks out, but the appliance still won't operate properly, a service call still may not be necessary. A competent service technician might be able to offer a suggestion by phone that could eliminate the trip entirely. Or, at the very least, the technician can come better prepared to remedy the problem—with a special repair part that may be needed, for example.

To handle the situation as quickly and efficiently as possible, do the following when you make the initial call to the service firm:

• Give clear, complete information, including what is wrong with the operation of the appliance and any unusual sounds or noises. If you have them, give the model and serial numbers and the approximate purchase date.

• After an inspection, ask for a cost estimate. It might be more cost-efficient to replace an older appliance needing major repair with a new one.

• Be prepared to show the service technician warranty information, if applicable. If the appliance is still under warranty, avoid trying to repair it yourself. You may nullify your right to free parts or labor.

• Most service firms will not make specific appointments because they are not sure how long each call will take. However, many will promise a morning or afternoon call. Also, some service firms are staggering their work hours to accommodate families where both the husband and wife work and persons who live alone.

• Clear the work area before the service technician arrives. This will cut down on the length of the service call and therefore save you money.

FINDING A SERVICE FIRM

During the warranty period, rely for service on the selling dealer or the service firm authorized to fulfill the warranty terms. After the warranty expires, use the same service firm or select a firm listed under the manufacturer's trademark heading in the Yellow Pages directory.

WHAT TO EXPECT FROM SERVICE

There are certain things every appliance owner has a right to expect from a service agency. These range from a knowledgeable service technician who's neat in appearance and courteous in manner to prompt action and an adequate supply of repair parts.

Trained Personnel Quality appliance manufacturers have established extensive dealer service training programs to ensure a continuing number of top-performing service technicians. These technicians are qualified to confidently diagnose the problem and make the necessary repairs.

Replacement Parts A service agency should stock an adequate supply of genuine replacement parts, have the latest tools and equipment for making repairs and include a sufficient number of well-equipped service vehicles.

Reputation The reputation of the service firm in the community is a good guide to the type of service the firm provides. Ask friends, neighbors or relatives for their opinions of the firm.

WHAT TO DO IF YOU'RE NOT SATISFIED WITH THE SERVICE OR WITH APPLIANCE PERFORMANCE

First, try to resolve the problems with the dealer who sold the appliance or the authorized firm which serviced it. If that doesn't work, contact the manufacturer. The address and perhaps a telephone number should be in the appliance manual or on the appliance.

If you're still not happy, you can take your complaint to the **Major Appliance Consumer Action Panel (MACAP)**. MACAP is an industry-sponsored but independent group of consumer representatives with expertise on both technical and consumer-action sides, who serve on a voluntary basis.

MACAP's address is: 20 North Wacker Drive, Chicago, IL 60606. When you write, include the following information: Your name, address and telephone number; the brand, model and serial number of your appliance; its purchase date and price; the name, address and phone number of the dealer or repair service; copies of all letters you have written or received about your complaint; copies of all service receipts; and a clear description of your problem with your recommendation for a reasonable solution.

AND A FINAL WORD ON SERVICE

Home service calls are expensive. But, good service doesn't just happen. The operation of a dependable service department requires organization, competent management and employees and usually a substantial capital investment.

Service technicians' salaries are only a part of the expense in making a service call. The labor charge or the profit on the repair parts also must cover the cost of training, service vehicles and maintenance, travel time, tools and test equipment and investment in repair parts. Other costs include maintaining an office and office personnel, lights, heat, telephone, rent, insurance, taxes, employee benefits, advertising, uniforms and uniform upkeep.

General Index

Recipe Index